SONGS OF
SCOTLAND

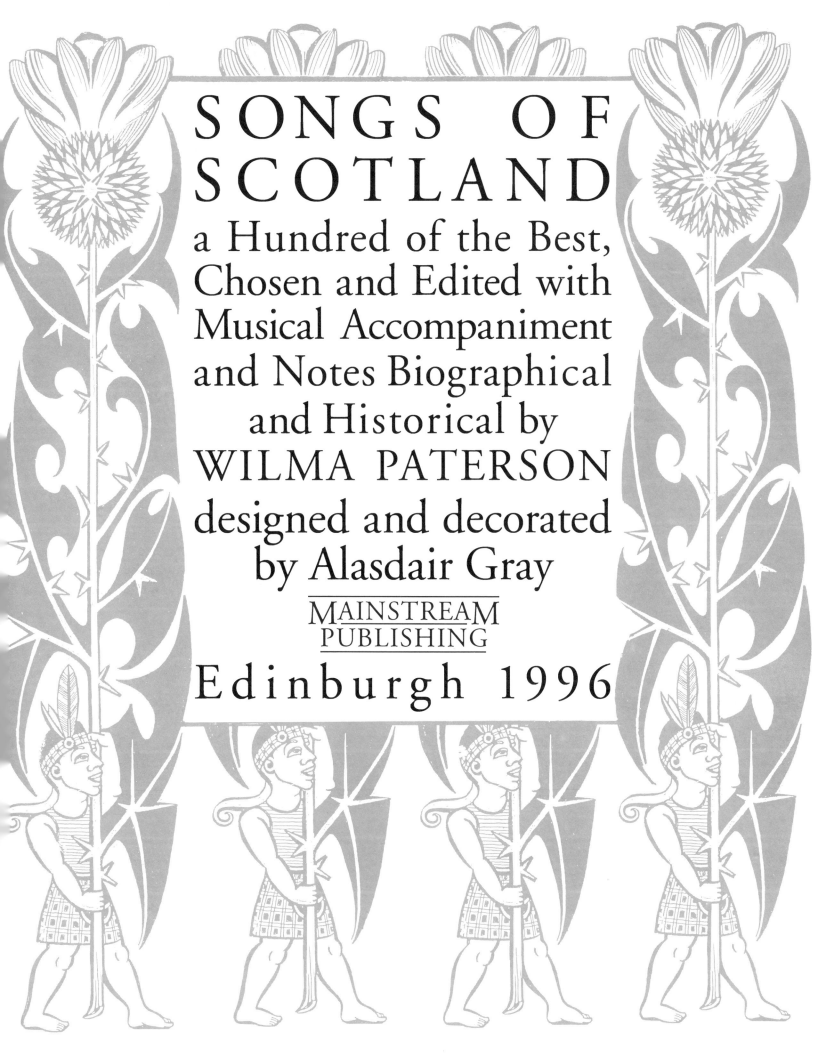

SONGS OF SCOTLAND

a Hundred of the Best,
Chosen and Edited with
Musical Accompaniment
and Notes Biographical
and Historical by
WILMA PATERSON
designed and decorated
by Alasdair Gray

MAINSTREAM
PUBLISHING

Edinburgh 1996

COPYRIGHT © WILMA PATERSON, 1996 (MUSIC AND TEXT)
© ALASDAIR GRAY, 1996 (ILLUSTRATIONS)
THE MORAL RIGHT OF THE AUTHOR HAS BEEN ASSERTED
ALL RIGHTS RESERVED

FIRST PUBLISHED IN GREAT BRITAIN 1996 BY
MAINSTREAM PUBLISHING COMPANY (EDINBURGH) LTD.
7 ALBANY STREET, EDINBURGH EH1 3UG

ISBN 1 85158 722 5
A CATALOGUE RECORD FOR THIS BOOK IS AVAILABLE
FROM THE BRITISH LIBRARY.

NO PART OF THIS BOOK MAY BE REPRODUCED OR TRANSMITTED
WITHOUT PERMISSION IN WRITING FROM THE PUBLISHER,
EXCEPT BY A REVIEWER QUOTING BRIEF PASSAGES
IN A MAGAZINE, NEWSPAPER OR BROADCAST.

SUBSIDISED BY
THE SCOTTISH **ARTS** COUNCIL

PRINTED BY BPC WHEATONS, EXETER

FOR ALLAN

INTRODUCTION

There is a certain irregularity in the old Scotch songs, a redundancy of syllables with respect to that exactness & measure that the English Poetry requires, but which glides in, most melodiously with the respective tunes to which they are set.

Robert Burns, *Commonplace Book,* September 1785.

THIS COLLECTION might never have seen the light of day had not ten-year-old Sophie Ramsay sung songs by Lady Nairne after dinner at Bamff House one summer evening in 1994. As in Lady Nairne's day Sophie sang unaccompanied. The rest of the company, fortified by a Noble whisky, gathered later round the piano to sing some old favourites which we feared had been slipping into oblivion in recent years. I am grateful to Sophie, to Janey Buchan who let me browse through and borrow from her marvellous library of folk music, and to Mary Anne Alburger for her patience and good humour while typesetting my complex manuscript. Mary Anne's job was made more difficult by additions and changes she was asked to make up to the last possible minute, and by the designer constantly pressing her to make the pages look simple despite the complicated typography. She obviously succeeded.

The hundred songs and ballads in this collection are a small sample of Scotland's wonderful treasury of traditional song – perhaps the richest in Europe. Making a selection was not easy, and of course my choice is a personal one. Until the 1960s most of these songs were familiar to Scots of every social class. We had learned them at school, they were sung in concerts and music halls and broadcast by the BBC Scottish Home Service. More importantly they were sung and played in the homes of amateur musicians who had learned them from their parents.

A TRADITION OF DESPAIR

Television changed all that, and Scots songs were gradually dropped from the curricula of most of our schools – either because the Scottish Education Department thought that anglicization offered the best start in life or because it was preparing for the economy measures which have made class singing a subject which Scottish schools need not teach, and now mostly don't.

So the number of people who get together at home and sing, play and revitalize the sort of music they learned at school or from their parents and each other is greatly reduced and these are the people on whom the music of a nation chiefly depends. But before mourning the death of a uniquely Scottish culture I'll quote some other pessimists.

. . . the Scots language is being lost every day and in a short time it will be unintelligible.
James Boswell, biographer, 1764

Time is crumbling down Scotland and England into – Britain. We may storm against this from p tforms, declaim passionately against it in "Lays of the Cavaliers," lift up our voices and weep over it in "Braemar Ballads," but necessity cares little for these things , and quietly does her work.
Alexander Smith, poet and essayist, 1865

Scotland is abandoning its once noble vernacular to the coarse usages of the vulgar, and generally adopting English manners and customs. Its language is fast becoming Anglicised, and this gradual absorption of the nation's individuality will prove a surer instrument of annihilation for Scottish song than did the clumsy pruning-axe of the Reformation . . .

Jessie Findlay, author, 1902

These three clear-sighted, patriotic authors believed that an independent Scottish culture – and therefore the songs which carry so much of it – was as near extinction in their day as it obviously is in ours. A short account of the sources of songs in this collection will explain why their judgement was premature. But first a word about the songs themselves.

THE OLDEST SONGS

At least half the songs in this collection are by that most prolific author of all, Anon. The ballads, which date back to the Middle Ages, are probably the oldest. Essentially dramatic and economic of description, they deal mainly with the powerful, universal themes of love, death and the supernatural. Some appeared in print in little 18th-century pamphlets called chapbooks, or as broadsides. Because of the ephemeral nature of these publications many must have been lost – even more so songs which were never published, and only existed in the elusive oral forms. Of those surviving, there are many local variants since the songs travelled to and from different parts of the country, the singers changing names of characters and places to make them more familiar to the audience.

'Scottish folk song,' wrote Edwin Muir, 'is pure feeling; but the ballads express a view of life which is essentially philosophic.' Ballads often relate, or appear to relate to historical events, and whether or not the events happened as narrated they tell more about human emotion and behaviour in a few verses than many historians convey in an entire volume.

But the chapbook ballads were not the only Scots folksongs printed in the 18th century. Books of them were sold to professional musicians and middle-class amateurs for drawing-room performances. Polite European society had hitherto aspired to the music of royal courts and the aristocracy. Every land had folksongs, of course, and in England, France and Germany before the 19th century folk music was left to the working class who produced it. In 1707 however, the Scottish middle classes were shocked into protective awareness of their folk culture by the union of the Scottish and English parliaments.

THE FIRST COLLECTORS

Most Scots hated it. There are no records of them complaining about the union of the crowns in 1603 when a Scots king went south to rule all Britain from London, but when their own parliament unexpectedly voted itself out of existence – when their elected leaders and landlords decided to rule them from London – they had a better reason for thinking Scotland dead than any generation since. A leader of the last Scots parliament called its extinction 'the end of an auld sang' but he was wrong. For when the Scots politicians went south they left behind a ruling class of lawyers, teachers and local lairds who *knew* they were not English and had a legal system, religion, literature and songs to prove it. Some resolved to cultivate these; others adopted English manners, hoping to profit by contact with their richer neighbour; and many tried to do both at the same time. One of these was Allan Ramsay.

An Edinburgh wigmaker turned bookseller, publisher and poet, his *Tea-Table Miscellany* of 1723 was a collection of Scots and English songs to be sung to existing tunes which he named without notating. This stimulated the first important collection I have drawn upon in this book. William Thomson's *Orpheus Caledonius* was the first Scottish song-book to be published with both words and music. It contained songs in two editions (1725 & 1733) which had never appeared in print before. Thomson was a London-based professional singer of Scottish descent whose delicately ornamented arrangements are extremely tasteful. Although most of the words were pirated from Ramsay's *Tea-Table Miscellany* we need not deplore this, for if piracy means 'using without permission of the originator' then Ramsay too was a pirate when he printed old songs which we label 'traditional'.

Ramsay altered some old songs till they were more his than anyone else's, thus starting a Scottish literary tradition which was a continuation of the oral one through the medium of print. Middle-class authors like Lady Nairne, Walter Scott and Robert Louis Stevenson – and working-class geniuses like Burns and James Hogg – wrote lyrics of their own to old melodies, and produced their own variants of ancient texts. These have been called 'pseudo-folksongs' but, since they are popular enough to be widely sung several generations after they were written, they are genuine folksongs.

The Scottish song-stream was not walled off from other nations. In his introduction to his collection of 18th-century lyrics Thomas Crawford says, 'Of the three thousand or so songs published in Scottish poetical miscellanies and song books from 1682 to 1785, some two thousand are in English, including many by Englishmen; and in the broadsides and chapbooks printed in Scotland for mass consumption during the century, about half the tales and songs seem to have been on English or Irish topics.' A healthy culture is strengthened, not weakened, by contact with others, as Scottish folk music was to demonstrate in the 20th century.

ROBERT BURNS

Nearly a quarter of the songs in this book are by Burns, but they are just a tiny part of an impressive and little-known œuvre. Burns wrote, revised or collected around three hundred and seventy songs. Robert Louis Stevenson was disappointed that in later life Burns 'rarely found courage for any more sustained effort than a song', but these great lyrics are now beginning to get the recognition they deserve.

Burns's love songs alone cover a huge spectrum, showing the tenderness of married love *(John Anderson My Jo)*, the bitterness of the jilted *(She's Fair and Fause)*, or the gratitude of the satisfied *(Corn Rigs)*. *My Tocher's the Jewel, I'm O'er Young to Marry Yet* and *Tam Glen* show uncanny insight into female psychology, while immortal love songs such as *Ae Fond Kiss* rub shoulders with unashamed celebrations of the pleasures of sex.

But apart from being an inspired songwriter, Burns was a folksong collector in the modern sense, who faithfully recorded both words and melodies of traditional songs. He also altered and 'improved' traditional material and if only a melody existed, or a mere fragment of a verse or chorus, he would write words to fit the character and mood of the music, substituting suitably polite ones for those of indecent traditional songs so that they could be sung in mixed company.

Always he specified which tune his verses should be sung to, and he was musically literate, with a neat, clear notation. His particular love was the unaccompanied female voice, but he played the fiddle and often set words to tunes which had until then been purely instrumental pieces – reels and strathspeys in particular. Some of these are extremely taxing to the singer. Burns wrote to his publisher Thomson, in September 1793,

. . . until I am compleat master of a tune, and in my own singing, (such as it is) I never can compose for it. – My way is: I consider the poetic Sentiment, correspondent to my idea of the musical expression; then chuse my theme; begin one Stanza; when that is composed, which is generally the most difficult part of the business, I walk out, sit down now & then, look out for objects in Nature around me that are in unison or harmony with the cogitations of my fancy & workings of my bosom; humming every now & then the air with the verses I have framed: when I feel my Muse beginning to jade, I retire to the solitary fireside of my study, & there commit my effusions to paper; swinging, at intervals, on the hind legs of my elbow-chair, by way of calling forth my own critical strictures, as my pen goes on. –

Most of Burns's original songs and those he collected were first published in *The Scots Musical Museum*, an ambitious six-volume Scots song project (1787–1803) to which the poet unstintingly devoted himself for almost ten years. Burns met its publisher, James Johnson, when Volume One was almost completed but thereafter became editor in all but name until he died in 1796. This work with its six hundred songs presented without musical ornamentation and just a simple bass line remains, as Burns predicted, the most valuable and comprehensive collection of Scots songs. He wrote to Johnson (with characteristic modesty) just a few weeks before he died:

Your work is a great one; & though, now that it is near finished, I see if we were to begin again, two or three things that might be mended, yet I will venture to prophesy, that to future ages your Publication will be the text book & standard of Scottish Song & Music.

Other Burns songs in this book come from George Thomson's *A Select Collection of Original Scotish Airs for the Voice,* a five-volume collection (1793–1818), to which the poet contributed about a hundred songs, as usual without thought of payment, as he wrote to the publisher:

As to any remuneration you may think my Songs either above, *or* below *price; for they shall be absolutely the one or the other. – In the honest enthusiasm with which I embark in your undertaking, to talk of money, wages, fee, hire, &. would be downright Sodomy of Soul!*

That was written by a great poet who was saving his wife and children from destitution by working as a low-grade civil servant after failing as a farmer. He was using his free time to make a free gift of his country's greatest art while sickening to death by rheumatic fever.

THE SONGS CONTINUE

Allan Ramsay and William Thomson had preserved and extended Scottish song through the 18th century. Burns and his publisher launched it with great additions into the 19th. Walter Scott and a whole team of contributors – Charles Sharpe and James Hogg among them – continued it in the voluminous *Minstrelsy of the Scottish Borders.* Through the last decades of the 19th century and the first of the 20th, folklorists and musicians like Frances Tolmie and Marjory Kennedy-Fraser visited the Highlands and Islands and added Gaelic song to the Scottish repertoire. Since the 1950s Hamish Henderson, working with the School of Scottish Studies in Edinburgh, has recorded a wealth of folksong kept alive by travelling folk and fishermen and farm labourers in the north-east, by colliers and factory hands and political campaigners in towns and cities everywhere. Before Hamish Henderson started work, genteel archivists thought songs generated by industrial communities were worthless because such communities hardly existed in the days of Burns and Scott. Henderson is a poet whose songs are sung at folk concerts with those of Ewan McColl, Burns and the still prolific Anon, thus continuing the tradition of Burns, Ramsay and the ancient makars.

For as Scotland's music halls and the BBC Scottish Home Service died before the light of television and while Scottish schools were throwing out or mislaying Scottish song, folk clubs were started by people who were dissatisfied with the mainstream of commercial music. The Scottish folk tradition is not parochial and was strengthened by contact with Irish and Breton song, American blues and country and western. Amateur musicians attracted big enough audiences to create professional folk groups such as The Corries and The Whistlebinkies or Gaelic rock groups like Runrig and Capercaillie. These draw heavily on Burns while following his examples, mingling old songs with contemporary harmonies.

It now appears that since 1707 Scottish culture has lived on the brink of annihilation. The songs survived because a few writers and many more musicians continued to feed a popular appetite – one which refuses to die though older people keep thinking it must. My own fear of that has been somewhat alleviated by work on this collection.

For reasons of space and coherence I have limited myself to material from the 18th and 19th centuries, leaving more recent songs in the Scottish folk idiom for another volume. The only exceptions are four popular songs from Roberton's *Songs of the Isles* (published in 1950) – but of course these, like all

Burns's songs and many by his contemporaries, are settings of traditional tunes.

Having shown that this collection is only the latest in a long line that has worked to maintain Scottish song, it only remains for me to hope it is the most successful.

ABOUT THE TEXTS

To give the flavour of the earliest printed versions I have kept the original punctuation, typography and spelling, apart from changing Burns's 'bony' to 'bonny' for obvious reasons. Two or three other small changes to ensure legibility are mentioned in accompanying notes. Where the oldest printed version of a song was slightly anglicized for the London market (as often happened in the 18th century) I have let it stand. There are many Scots accents: highland and lowland, east coast and west, broad and genteel. Singers should use the accent they feel happiest with.

Where 19th-century editions abbreviated, bowdlerized or modernized 18th-century texts I have restored missing and 'corrected' stanzas. Where the original song has been superseded by another setting of the same words I have given both melodies. When new words have been set to existing tunes I have quoted both versions where space permits, as when Burns provided polite words for a traditional bawdy song, or sexually explicit words for a love song of his own for use in strictly male company. Each version has its unique merits. Many people will enjoy both.

ABOUT THE MUSIC

Some of the songs have been transposed to make them more accessible to the average singer, but I have retained 18th-century appoggiaturas and other decorations. I have not added any dynamic markings but have given brief indications for tempo, and occasionally expression, as a rough guide to interpretation. In rendering a Scots song, choice of tempo and dynamic (and the use of the sustaining pedal) is a matter for individual taste. The same tune may be sung fast or slow with equal validity – the singer's feeling for the words is the important thing. I have kept the accompaniments simple, so as not to damage the purity of the melodies, while providing a light support for the voice. Scots songs, however, are notoriously awkward to harmonize according to classical rules and are sometimes best sung unaccompanied, as was often the case in Burns's and Lady Nairne's day:

'The ladies of Edinburgh', wrote Henry Mackenzie, 'used to sing these airs without any accompaniment (indeed they scarce admitted of counterpoint, or any but a slight and delicate accompaniment) at tea and after supper, their position at table not being interrupted as now by rising to the pianoforte.' So I have dispensed with the introductory piano 'symphonies' characteristic of so many inappropriate 19th-century arrangements. In most cases the final bars may be played as an introduction and to establish the key.

Many Scots songs are extremely awkward to sing – I know at least one highly successful opera singer who will do anything rather than render one in public. Octave leaps and other hazardous intervals are commonplace, and the range can be cruelly wide, which is one reason why I have incorporated the melody in the right hand of the piano part – the player can maintain the tune when the voice disappears. It also provides complete little piano pieces for players of modest technique. In the 18th century many Scots tunes were used by upper-class children for instrumental practice.

Most songs in this book can be played on fiddle, guitar, flute or other instrument, and the simple bass line on cello. There is no sharp division between vocal and instrumental music in traditional Scots music since fiddlers borrowed and altered songs while singers often put words to fiddle tunes. The mobility of this tradition has allowed Scottish folksong to persist and renew itself up to the present day, despite the multinational entertainment industries which ignore it. But what the tradition has gained in the 20th century should be left to another volume.

Meanwhile, those who want to examine the sources of Scottish music for themselves will find the following books as useful as I did.

Wilma Paterson, Glasgow, 1996

AIRD, JAMES. *A Selection of Scotch, English, Irish, and Foreign Airs.* 6 vols. Glasgow, 1782–1803

BOULTON, HAROLD ed. *Songs of the North.* London, 1895

BREMNER, ROBERT. *Airs and Marches.* Edinburgh, 1756–61
A Collection of Scots Reels or Country Dances. London, c. 1765

BRONSON, BERTRAND HARRIS. *The Traditional Tunes of the Child Ballads.* 4 vols. Princeton, 1959–66

BUCHAN, NORMAN. *101 Scottish Songs.* Glasgow and London, 1962

CHILD, F. J. *The English & Scottish Popular Ballads.* 5 vols. London, 1882–98

CRAWFORD, THOMAS. *Burns: A Study of the Poems and Songs.* Edinburgh, 1960
Love, Labour and Liberty: The Eighteenth Century Scottish Lyric. Cheadle, Cheshire, 1976

CROMEK, R. H. *Select Scottish Songs.* 1810

DICK, JAMES C. *The Songs of Robert Burns.* London, 1903
Notes on Scottish Songs by Robert Burns, 1908

D'URFEY, THOMAS. *Pills to Purge Melancholy.* London, 1718

EYRE-TODD, GEORGE. *Ancient Scots Ballads.* Glasgow and London, 1894

FINDLAY, JESSIE P. *The Spindle-Side of Scottish Song.* London, 1902

FORD, ROBERT. *Vagabond Songs and Ballads of Scotland.* London, 1899

GLEADHILL, T. S. *Kyle's Scottish Lyric Gems.* Glasgow, 1880

GOW, NIEL. *A Collection of Strathspey Reels.* Edinburgh, 1784

HERD, DAVID. *Ancient and Modern Scottish Songs, Heroic Ballads etc.* Edinburgh, 1776

HOGG, JAMES. *Jacobite Reliques.* 2 vols. Edinburgh, 1819–21

JOHNSON, DAVID. *Music and Society in Lowland Scotland in the Eighteenth Century.* Oxford, 1973

JOHNSON, JAMES. *The Scots Musical Museum.* 6 vols. Edinburgh, 1787–1803

LOW, DONALD A. *The Songs of Robert Burns.* London, 1993

LYLE, EMILY. *Scottish Ballads.* Edinburgh, 1994

MACKENZIE, HENRY. *The Anecdotes and Egotisms of Henry Mackenzie, 1745–1831,* ed. Harold W. Thompson. London, 1927

MACQUOID, G. S. ed. *Jacobite Songs & Ballads.* London, 1887

MOFFAT, ALFRED. *The Minstrelsy of Scotland.* London, 1896
The Minstrelsy of the Scottish Highlands. London, n. d.

NAPIER, WILLIAM. *A Selection of the Most Favourite Scots Songs.* London, 1790

OSWALD, JAMES. *The Caledonian Pocket Companion.* 12 vols. London, c. 1743–60
A Curious Collection of Scots Tunes. Edinburgh, c. 1740

PLAYFORD, HENRY. *A Collection of Original Scotch-Tunes, (Full of the Highland Humours).* London, 1700

RAMSAY, ALLAN ed. *The Tea-Table Miscellany. A Collection of Choice Songs.* Edinburgh, 1724–40

ROBINSON, MAIRI ed. *The Concise Scots Dictionary.* Aberdeen, 1985

SCOTT, WALTER. *Minstrelsy of the Scottish Border.* 3 vols. Kelso, 1802–3

SMITH, R. A. *The Scottish Minstrel.* 1820–24

STENHOUSE, WILLIAM. *Illustrations of the Lyric Poetry and Music of Scotland.* Edinburgh, 1853

THOMSON, GEORGE ed. *A Select Collection of Original Scotish Airs for the Voice.* 5 vols. 1793–1818

THOMSON, WILLIAM. *Orpheus Caledonius: A Collection of Scots Songs Set to Music.* London, 1725, 1733

TABLE OF

SO IT'S WAR!

SCOTS, WHA HAE WI' WALLACE BLED   2
Robert Burns   *Tune: Hey Tutti Taitie*

PIBROCH OF DONUIL DHU   4
Sir Walter Scott   *Tune: Pibroch of Donuil Dubh*

THE CAMPBELLS ARE COMIN, OHO! OHO!   6
Robert Burns   *Tune as in title*

JOHNNIE COPE   8
Adam Skirving   *Tune as in title*

ORAN AN T-SAIGHDEIR   10
THE SOLDIER'S SONG
Major Neil MacLeod
Traditional tune as sung by Patrick MacLeod

MY LOVE'S IN GERMANIE   12
Hector Macneil   *Tune as in title*

BONNIE DUNDEE   14
Sir Walter Scott   *Tune as in title*

LADS WANT LASSIES

DUNCAN GRAY   Robert Burns   18
WEARY FA' YOU DUNCAN GRAY
Robert Burns   *Tune as in 2nd title*

HO RO MO NIGHEAN DONN   20
BHOIDHEACH   Traditional Gaelic
HO-RO MY NUT-BROWN MAIDEN
Dr Blackie's Translation   *Tune as in 1st title*

KELVIN GROVE   22
Thomas Lyle   *Tune: O the Shearin's No for You*

MARY MORISON   Robert Burns   24
Two tunes: *The Miller* and *Duncan Davison*

THY CHEEK IS O' THE ROSE'S HUE   26
Richard Gall   *Tune: My Only Jo and Dearie, O*

AY, WAUKIN, O   Robert Burns   *Tune as in title*   28

WILT THOU BE MY DEARIE?   30
Robert Burns   *Tune: The Sutor's Dochter*

CA' THE YOWES TO THE KNOWES   32
Two versions by Robert Burns   *Tune as in title*

TURN YE TO ME   John Wilson (Christopher   34
North)   AIR FEASGAR CIUIN CEITEIN
Traditional Gaelic   *Tune as in 2nd title*

THE BIRKS OF ABERFELDY   Robert Burns   36
THE BIRKS O' ABERGELDIE
Traditional   *Tune as in 2nd title*

MY BOY TAMMY   Hector Macneil   38
Tune as in title

LANG HAE WE PARTED BEEN   40
Robert Burns   *Tune: Laddie Lie Near Me*

BONNIE CHARLIE

THERE'LL NEVER BE PEACE TILL JAMIE   42
COMES HAME   Robert Burns
Tune: There Are Few Good Fellows When Jamie's Awa

HIGHLAND LADDIE   Charles Walker, and   44
Traditional   *Tune as in title*

COME O'ER THE STREAM, CHARLIE   46
James Hogg   *Tune as in title*

CHARLIE IS MY DARLING   Lady Nairne   48
CHARLIE, HE'S MY DARLING   Robert Burns
Tune as in 2nd title

WILL YE NO COME BACK AGAIN?   50
Lady Nairne   *Tune as in title*

SPEED BONNIE BOAT   Sir Harold Boulton   52
OVER THE SEA TO SKYE   R. L. Stevenson
Tune: Highland rowing song

CONTENTS

O, I AM COME TO THE LOW COUNTRIE 54
Robert Burns   *Tune: Ochon, Ochon, Ochrie!*

LASSIES WANT LADS

THA MI SGITH   Traditional Gaelic 56
WHY SHOULD I SIT AND SIGH?
James Hogg   *Tune: Eilidh Bhan*

I LOVE MY LOVE IN SECRET   Traditional 58
Tune as in title

ROBIN ADAIR   Traditional 60
Tune: Ceud mìle failte, Eilean mo rùin

TAM GLEN   Robert Burns 62
MY DADDY'S A DELVER OF DYKES
Traditional   *Tune as in 2nd title*

THE BROOM OF COWDENKNOWS 64
Traditional   *Tune as in title*

GLENOGIE   Traditional   *Tune as in title* 66

MY MITHER'S AY GLOW'RIN OWRE ME 68
Allan Ramsay   *Tune: A Health to Betty*

JOCK O' HAZELDEAN 70
Sir Walter Scott   *Tune as in title*

SKULDUGGERY AND SUDDEN DEATH

THE BONNIE EARL O' MURRAY 74
Traditional   *Two tunes, one by William Thomson*

THE TWA CORBIES 76
Traditional   *Two tunes: 1st as in title, 2nd Breton melody, An Alarc'h (The Swan)*

JOHNY FAA *OR* THE GYPSIE LADDIE 78
Traditional   *Tune as in title*

THE BONNIE HOUSE O' AIRLIE 80
Two traditional versions   *Tune as in title*

BONNIE GEORGE CAMPBELL 83
Traditional   *Tune as in title*

WILLY'S RARE AND WILLY'S FAIR 84
Traditional   *Tune as in title*

O THAT I WERE WHERE HELEN LIES 86
Traditional   *Tune as in title*

LORD RONALD   Traditional   *Tune as in title* 88

McPHERSON'S FAREWELL 90
Robert Burns   *Tune as in title*

A HIGHLAND LAD MY LOVE WAS BORN 92
Robert Burns   THE WHITE COCKADE
Traditional   *Tune: as in 2nd title*

YOUNG WATERS   Traditional 94
Tune as in title

SIR PATRICK SPENCE 96
Traditional   *Tune as in title*

FINE FLOWERS IN THE VALLEY 98
Traditional   *Tune as in title*

LOVE SATISFIED

GREEN GROW THE RASHES, O 100
Two versions by Robert Burns
Tune as in title

AS I CAME O'ER THE CAIRNEY MOUNT 102
Robert Burns, with impolite earlier version
Tune as in title

O MY LUVE'S LIKE A RED, RED ROSE 104
Robert Burns   *Tune: Major Graham*

GRADH GEAL MO CHRIDH 106
Traditional Gaelic, as sung by Mary MacInnes
ERISKAY LOVE LILT   Marjory Kennedy-Fraser's version   *Tune as in 1st title*

TABLE OF

FLOW GENTLY, SWEET AFTON 108
Robert Burns *Tune: Afton Water*

DAINTY DAVIE Traditional, with impolite 110
version by Robert Burns *Tune as in title*

CORN RIGS Robert Burns
CORN RIGGS ARE BONNY Allan Ramsay 112
Tune as in title

LOVE DOOMED OR REJECTED

THE GREAT SELCHIE OF SULE SKERRY 116
Traditional *Two tunes as in title*

THE FLOWERS OF THE FOREST 118
Two versions: Jean Elliot and Alison Rutherford
Tune as in title

GILDEROY Traditional *Tune as in title* 120

BONNY BARBARA ALLAN 122
Traditional *Tune as in title*

THE WINTER IT IS PAST 124
Robert Burns *Tune as in title*

O WALY, WALY UP YON BANK 126
Traditional *Tune as in title*

THE FOUR MARIES 127
Traditional *Tune as in title*

YE BANKS AND BRAES 128
O' BONNIE DOON Robert Burns
Tune: The Caledonian Hunt's Delight

AE FOND KISS Robert Burns 130
Two tunes: Rory Dall's Port and a strathspey

THE BONNIE BANKS 132
O' LOCH LOMOND
Traditional, with version by Lady John Scott
Tune: Kind Robin Lo'es Me

MY LOVE, SHE'S BUT A LASSIE YET 134
Robert Burns MY LOVE SHE'S BUT A
LASSIE YET James Hogg *Tune as in titles*

I'M O'ER YOUNG TO MARRY YET 136
Robert Burns *Tune as in title*

SHE'S FAIR AND FAUSE THAT CAUSES 138
MY SMART Robert Burns *Tune: The Lads of Leith*

MY TOCHER'S THE JEWEL 140
Robert Burns *Tune: The Highway to Edinburgh*

WEDDINGS – LULLABIES – MARRIAGE

THE LAIRD O' COCKPEN Lady Nairne 144
WHEN SHE CAM BEN SHE BOBBED
Traditional *Tune as in 2nd title*

THE TINKLERS' WADDIN' William Watt 146
ROTHESAY, O Anon *Tune as in 2nd title*

LEEZIE LINDSAY Traditional *Tune as in title* 150

MAIRI'S WEDDING Sir Hugh S. Roberton 152
Tune as in title

O CAN YE SEW CUSHIONS? 154
Traditional *Tune as in title*

CAGARAN GAOLACH Traditional Gaelic 156
HUSH YE, MY BAIRNIE
Malcolm Macfarlane *Tune as in 1st title*

AN COINEACHAN Traditional Gaelic 158
A FAIRY LULLABY Lachlan Macbean's
translation *Tune as in 1st title*

COULTER'S CANDY 160
Robert Coltart *Tune as in title*

LEANABH AN AIGH Mary Macdonald 162
CHILD IN THE MANGER
Lachlan Macbean's translation *Tune: Bunessan*

CONTENTS

JOHN GRUMLIE   Traditional   164
THE WIFE OF AUCHTERMUCHTY
American version   *Tune as in 2nd title*

O AN YE WERE DEAD, GUDEMAN   168
Traditional
THERE WAS A LAD WAS BORN IN KYLE
Robert Burns   *Tune as in 1st title*

JOHN ANDERSON MY JO   Robert Burns   170
and impolite traditional version
Tune as in title

EXILE

THE GLOOMY NIGHT IS GATH'RING FAST   174
Robert Burns   *Tune: The House of Glams*

THE SCOTTISH EMIGRANT'S FAREWELL   176
Alexander Hume   *Tune as in title*

WANDERING WILLIE   Robert Burns   178
2nd version by R. L. Stevenson   *Tune as in title*

THE SUN RISES BRIGHT IN FRANCE   180
Allan Cunningham   *Tune as in title*

MY HEART'S IN THE HIGHLANDS   182
Robert Burns   *Two tunes: Crodh Chailein and
The Musket Salute*

JOY OF MY HEART   Sir Hugh S. Roberton   184
EILEAN MO CHRIDH   John R. Bannerman's
version   *Tune as in 2nd title*

CHI MI NA MOR-BHEANNA   John Cameron   186
THE MIST-COVERED MOUNTAINS
OF HOME   Malcolm Macfarlane   *Tune as in title*

MINGULAY BOAT SONG   188
Sir Hugh S. Roberton   *Tune as in title*

THE ROWAN TREE   190
Lady Nairne   *Tune as in title*

FAREWELL TO FIUNARY   192
Dr Norman Macleod
SORAIDH SLAN LE FIONNAIRIDH!
Translation by Archibald Sinclair
Tune: Irinn oirinn o horo

COME ALL YE !

THE PIPER O' DUNDEE   196
Traditional   *Tune as in title*

THE DEIL CAM FIDDLIN THRO' THE   198
TOWN   Robert Burns   *Tune: The Hemp-dresser*

ISLAND SPINNING SONG   200
Sir Hugh S. Roberton   *Tune as in title*

CHAIDH NA FIR A SGATHABHAIG   202
The Men Have Gone to Scavaig
Traditional Gaelic   *Tune: Skye waulking song*

CALLER HERRIN'   204
Lady Nairne   *Tune as in title*

A MAN'S A MAN FOR A' THAT   206
Robert Burns   *Tune: For A' That*

THE LAND O' THE LEAL   208
Lady Nairne   *Tune: Hey Tutti Taitie*

AMAZING GRACE   210
John Newton   *Tune as in title*

AULD LANG SYNE

AULD LANG SYNE   214
Robert Burns   *with 2 tunes, both called
Auld Lang Syne*

INDEX OF TITLES AND FIRST LINES   217

SO IT'S WAR!

SCOTS, WHA HAE WI' WALLACE BLED

March-like

con Ped.

Scots, wha hae wi' Wal - lace bled, Scots, wham Bruce has aft - en led,___

Wel - come to your go - ry bed Or to vic - tor - ie!

Now's the day and now's the hour; See the front o' bat - tle lour,

See ap - proach proud Ed - ward's pow'r Chains and sla - ve - rie!

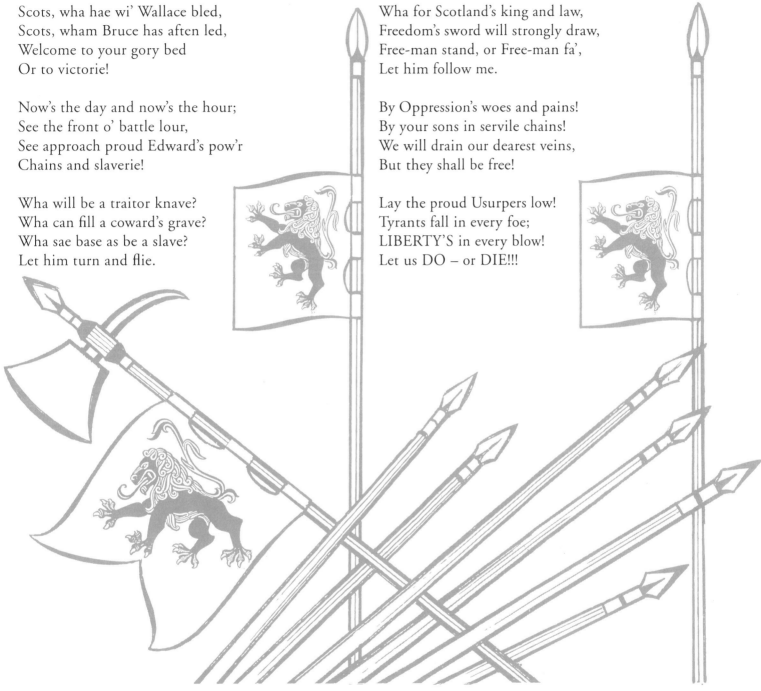

Scots, wha hae wi' Wallace bled,
Scots, wham Bruce has aften led,
Welcome to your gory bed
Or to victorie!

Now's the day and now's the hour;
See the front o' battle lour,
See approach proud Edward's pow'r
Chains and slaverie!

Wha will be a traitor knave?
Wha can fill a coward's grave?
Wha sae base as be a slave?
Let him turn and flie.

Wha for Scotland's king and law,
Freedom's sword will strongly draw,
Free-man stand, or Free-man fa',
Let him follow me.

By Oppression's woes and pains!
By your sons in servile chains!
We will drain our dearest veins,
But they shall be free!

Lay the proud Usurpers low!
Tyrants fall in every foe;
LIBERTY'S in every blow!
Let us DO – or DIE!!!

'DIE!!!' rhymes Scottishly with 'free', of course. So does 'flie'. In 1787 Robert Burns visited Bannockburn and was deeply affected, writing to Robert Muir on August 16: 'I knelt at the tomb of Sir John Graham, the gallant friend of the immortal Wallace; and two hours ago I said a fervent prayer for Old Caledonia over the hole in a blue whinstone, where Robert de Bruce fixed his royal standard on the banks of Bannockburn.' Burns thought much later of celebrating Bruce and his great victory, and the old tune 'Hey Tutti Taitie' came to mind: 'Well I know that, with Fraser's Hautboy, it has often filled my eye with tears. There is a tradition, which I have met with in many places in Scotland, that it was Robert Bruce's March at the battle of Bannock-burn. – This thought, in my yesternight's evening walk, warmed me to a pitch of enthusiasm on the theme of Liberty & Independence, which I threw into a kind of Scots Ode, fitted to the air that one might suppose to be the gallant ROYAL SCOT's address to his heroic followers on that eventful morning.'

CHORUS REPEATS LAST 4 LINES OF EACH VERSE

Pibroch of Donuil Dhu,
Pibroch of Donuil,
Wake thy wild voice anew,
Summon Clan Conuil;
Come away, come away,
Hark to the summons!
Come in your war array,
Gentles and commons!
Come away, come away,
Hark to the summons!
Come in your war array,
Gentles and commons.

Come from deep glen, and
From mountains so rocky,
War pipe and pennon
Are at Inverlochy;
Come ev'ry hill-plaid, and
True heart that wears one,
Come ev'ry steel blade, and
Strong hand that bears one!

Leave untended the herd,
The flock without shelter;
Leave the corpse uninterr'd,
The bride at the altar;
Leave the deer, leave the steer,
Leave nets and barges;
Come with your fighting gear,
Broadsword, and targes!

Come as the winds come, when
Forests are rended;
Come as the waves come, when
Navies are stranded;
Faster come, faster come,
Faster and faster;
Chief, vassal, page, and groom,
Tenant and master!

Fast they come, fast they come,
See how they gather!
Wide waves the eagle plume,
Blended with heather.
Cast your plaids, draw your blades,
Forward each man set!
Pibroch o' Donuil Dhu
Knell for the onset!
Cast your plaids, draw your blades,
Forward each man set!
Pibroch o' Donuil Dhu
Knell for the onset!

The tune appeared in Oswald's Caledonian Pocket Companion, *Bk. XII c. 1764 ('Pioberachd Mhic Dhonuil'), but Sir Walter Scott's verses were written later and published in* Albyn's Anthology, *c. 1816. The pipe tune 'Pibroch of Donuil Dubh' is associated with Clan Cameron and Clan Donald. Cameron history names it after Donald Dubh, traditionally the eleventh Chief from about 1400–1460. Under him the Lochaber tribes emerged as an organized clan, and from him Cameron chiefs to this day inherit the well-known patronymic 'MacDhomhnuill Dhuibh' or Son of Black Donald.*

THE CAMPBELLS ARE COMIN, OHO! OHO!

Briskly

The Camp-bells are com-in, O-ho, O-ho! The Camp-bells are com-in, O-ho, O-ho! The

con Ped.

Fine

Camp-bells are com-in to bon-nie Loch-Lev-en, The Camp-bells are com-in, O-ho, O-ho!

Up-on the Lo-monds I lay, I lay,— Up-on the Lo-monds I lay, I lay, I

D.C.

look-ed down to bon-nie Loch-Lev-en And saw— three bon-nie perch-es play.

The Campbells are comin, Oho, Oho!
The Campbells are comin, Oho, Oho!
The Campbells are comin to bonnie LochLeven,
The Campbells are comin, Oho, Oho!

Upon the Lomonds I lay, I lay,
Upon the Lomonds I lay, I lay,
I looked down to bonnie LochLeven
And saw three bonnie perches play.

The Campbells are comin, Oho, Oho!
The Campbells are comin, Oho, Oho!
The Campbells are comin to bonnie LochLeven,
The Campbells are comin, Oho, Oho!

The great Argyle, he goes before,
He makes the cannons and guns to roar,
Wi' sound o' trumpet, pipe and drum
The Campbells are comin, Oho! Oho!

The Campbells are comin, Oho, Oho!
The Campbells are comin, Oho, Oho!
The Campbells are comin to bonnie LochLeven,
The Campbells are comin, Oho, Oho!

The Campbells they are a' in arms,
Their loyal faith and truth to show,
Wi' banners rattling in the wind
The Campbells are comin, Oho! Oho!

The Campbells are comin, Oho, Oho!
The Campbells are comin, Oho, Oho!
The Campbells are comin to bonnie LochLeven,
The Campbells are comin, Oho, Oho!

Clan Campbell occupied Argyll, the biggest mountainous landmass in south-west Scotland. Before and after the union of the crowns, kings in Edinburgh and London contrived to divide and rule the northern clans by strengthening the Campbells against their neighbours. From the days of Flodden onward this put the earls and dukes of Argyll among the most powerful subjects in the kingdom, a position they maintained until the present century despite occasional miscalculations. The 5th earl, though a supporter of John Knox, led Mary Queen of Scots's troops after her escape from Loch Leven castle. Some think this song refers to that. The popular tune opposite, with the title Burns used as his first line, is Jacobite, and traditionally associated with the 1715 Jacobite rebellion. However, the 8th and 9th earls were beheaded for disloyalty to the Stewarts and the 10th, after being made a duke by William of Orange, moved his loyalty to the Hanoverians by crushing the 1715 uprising for George the 1st. The 'loyal faith' celebrated in the last verse is probably the loyalty of the Campbells to their hereditary landlord rather than to a particular monarch. The tune is in Oswald's Caledonian Pocket Companion *(c .1751) and Bremner's* Reels *(1761). It appears with Burns's verses in* The Scots Musical Museum *of 1790 (vol. III, no. 299) – though his name is not attached.*

JOHNNIE COPE

March time

con Ped.

Cope— sent a chal- lenge— frae Dun- bar, Say- ing 'Char- lie meet— me—

an'— ye— daur, An' I'll learn ye the art o' war, If ye'll meet me in— the—

morn— ing.' Hey! John- nie Cope,— are ye wauk- in'— yet? Or—

are your drums a - beat- ing— yet? If— ye— were— wauk- in'—

I wad wait, Tae gang tae the coals in the morn - ing.

CHORUS AFTER EACH VERSE

Cope sent a challenge frae Dunbar,
Saying 'Charlie meet me an' ye daur,   *if you dare*
An' I'll learn ye the art o' war,
If ye'll meet me in the morning.'

Hey! Johnnie Cope, are ye waukin' yet?   *wakened*
Or are your drums a-beating yet?
If ye were waukin' I wad wait,
Tae gang tae the coals in the morning.

When Charlie looked the letter upon,
He drew his sword the scabbard from,
Come, follow me, my merry men,
And we'll meet Johnnie Cope in the morning.

Now Johnnie be as good as your word,
Come, let us try baith fire and sword,
And dinna flee like a frichted bird,   *frightened*
That's chased frae its nest i' the morning.

Fye now, Johnnie, get up an' rin,   *and run*
The Highland bagpipes mak' a din,
It's better tae sleep in a hale skin,   *whole*
For it will be a bluidie morning.

When Johnnie Cope tae Dunbar cam,
They speired at him, 'Where's a' your men?'   *asked*
'The de'il confound me gin I ken,
For I left them a' in the morning.'

Now Johnnie, troth ye werena blate,   *weren't modest*
Tae come wi' news o' your ain defeat,
An' leave your men in sic a strait,
Sae early in the morning.

In faith, quo Johnnie, I got sic flegs   *such blows*
Wi' their claymores an' philabegs,
Gin I face them again, de'il brak my legs,
So I wish you a' good morning.

General Sir John Cope has the doubtful distinction of being one of the most derided names in Scots history. He was Commander-in-Chief of Government troops at the start of the Jacobite rising in 1745 and took the field against Prince Charlie's army. While camped at Prestonpans Cope was attacked at dawn by the Jacobites led by Robert Anderson, who knew the ground well from snipe shooting. Cope lost his entire infantry but he himself managed to escape with some of the cavalry, and his notoriously cowardly arrival in Berwick was commemorated almost immediately in song by Adam Skirving, a farmer from near Haddington. Cope was, it was said at the time, 'the first general in Europe to bring the first tidings of his own defeat.' Burns produced a version for the Scots Musical Museum (vol. III, no. 234) but did not care for the tune which he thought suffered from 'a squalidity, an absence of elegance'. The pipe march Johnnie Cope is played at Reveille by most of the Scottish regiments – including the two in which the discredited General Cope served.

'N uair bhios mo chàirdean 'nan cadal,
Air an leabaidh gu sàmhach,
'S ann bhios mis' anns an oidhche,
Fò an choill aig mo nàmhaid;
Fò an choill aig mo nàmhaid,
Feadh mhachraichean còmhnard,
Feadh bheanntanan àrda,
Agus fàsaichean ceòthach.

(When my kindred are slumbering peacefully in bed, I shall be at night in hiding from my enemy, amid level plains, lofty mountains, and wildernesses enveloped in mist.) 'For several months every one in our glen sang and hummed this song, whilst at work', wrote Frances Tolmie (1840–1926) of Skye, who collected many of the island's folksongs. This one was taken down from the singing of a young Skye shepherd, Patrick MacLeod, but the words are by a Major Neil MacLeod of Waternish. The song was very popular on the island around the time of the Crimean war.

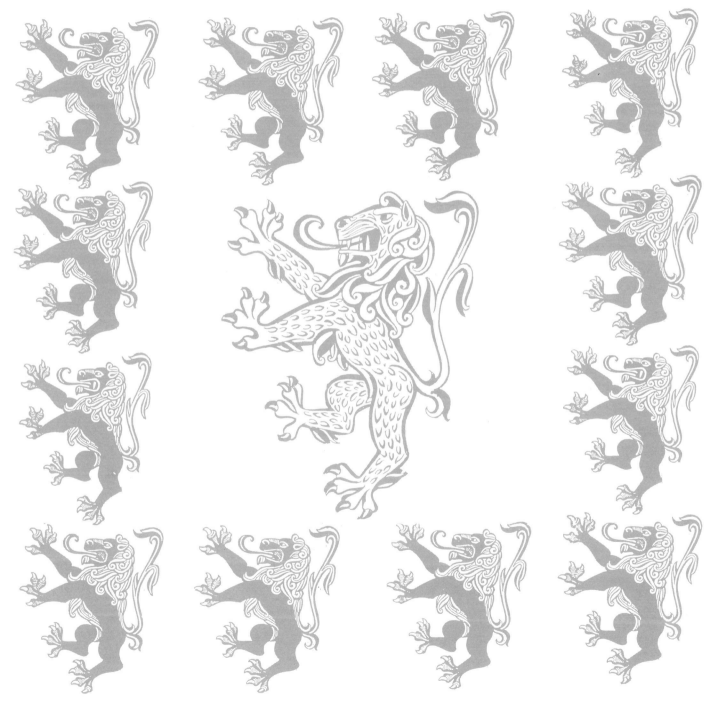

Moderately slow

con Ped.

My love's in Ger - man - ie, Send him hame, send him hame; My

love's in Ger - man - ie,____ send him hame! My____ love's in Ger - man - ie, Fight - ing

brave for roy - al - ty; He may ne'er his Jean - nie see;____ Send him

hame, send him hame; He may ne'er his Jean - nie see,____ send him hame.

My love's in Germanie,
Send him hame, send him hame;
My love's in Germanie, send him hame!
My love's in Germanie,
Fighting brave for royalty;
He may ne'er his Jeannie see;
Send him hame, send him hame;
He may ne'er his Jeannie see, send him hame.

He's brave as brave can be,
Send him hame, send him hame;
He's brave as brave can be, send him hame!
He's brave as brave can be,
He wad rather fa' than flee,
But his life is dear to me,
Send him hame, send him hame;
But his life is dear to me, send him hame!

His faes are ten to three,   *foes*
Send him hame, send him hame;
His faes are ten to three, send him hame!
His faes are ten to three,
He maun either fa' or flee;
In the cause o' loyalty
Send him hame, send him hame;
In the cause o' loyalty send him hame!

Your love ne'er learnt to flee,
Bonnie dame, winsome dame;
Your love ne'er learnt to flee, winsome dame!
Your love ne'er learnt to flee,
But he fell in Germanie
Fighting brave for royalty,
Bonnie dame, mournfu' dame;
Fighting brave for royalty, mournfu' dame!

He'll ne'er come owre the sea,
Willie's slain, Willie's slain;
He'll ne'er come owre the sea, Willie's gane!
He'll ne'er come owre the sea
To his love and ain countree;
This world's nae mair for me,
Willie's gane, Willie's gane;
This world's nae mair for me, Willie's slain!

This melody appears in the Scots Musical Museum *(no. 371) with traditional Jacobite words revised by Burns ('Ye Jacobites by name, give an ear, give an ear!') and it is also given in Hogg's* Jacobite Reliques *(1819–21) with the verses 'Ken ye how to fight a Whig, Aikendrum, Aikendrum?' This setting by Hector Macneil became popular in the 19th century but Burns's 'pithy ironical satire couched in equivocal terms which may be read by either Whig or Tory' is still sung with passion and vigour in Glasgow pubs. It has been suggested that the tune might be English although Moffat (* The Minstrelsy of Scotland, 1896) *refers to* The Complaynt of Scotland *(1549) which mentions a song entitled 'My lupe is lyand seik, sent hym ioy, sent hym ioy', which is possibly the original ballad. In 19th-century versions the sharpened 7th note (G sharp) is given as G natural. Macneil (1746–1818) wrote a good deal of poetry, many songs and other miscellaneous works after he returned to his native Scotland from the West Indies where he had been involved in the slave trade.*

Lively

con Ped.

To the Lords of Con - ven - tion 'twas Cla - ver'se who spoke, 'Ere the

King's crown shall fall there are crowns to be broke; So let each Ca - va - lier who loves

ho - nour and me, Come fol - low the bon - net o' Bon - nie Dun - dee.' *Come*

fill up my cup,— come fill up my can, Come sad - dle your hor - ses, and call up your men; Come

o- pen the West Port, and let me gang free, And it's room for the bon- nets o' Bon- nie Dun- dee!

CHORUS AFTER EACH VERSE

To the Lords of Convention 'twas Claver'se who spoke,
'Ere the King's crown shall fall there are crowns to be broke;
So let each Cavalier who loves honour and me,
Come follow the bonnet of Bonnie Dundee.'

Come fill up my cup, come fill up my can,
Come saddle your horses, and call up your men;
Come open the West Port and let me gang free,
And it's room for the bonnets of Bonnie Dundee!

Dundee he is mounted, he rides up the street,
The bells are rung backward, the drums they are beat;
But the Provost, douce man, said, 'Just e'en let him be,   *pleasant*
The Gude Town is weel quit of that Deil of Dundee.'

As he rode down the sanctified bends of the Bow,
Ilk carline was flyting and shaking her pow;   *old woman/ scolding/ head*
But the young plants of grace they look'd couthie and slee,
Thinking, 'Luck to thy bonnet, thou Bonnie Dundee!'

With sour-featured Whigs the Grassmarket was cramm'd
As if half the West had set tryst to be hang'd;
There was spite in each look, there was fear in each e'ee,
As they watch'd for the bonnets of Bonnie Dundee.

These cowls of Kilmarnock had spits and had spears,
And lang-hafted gullies to kill Cavaliers;
But they shrunk to close-heads, and the causeway was free,
At the toss of the bonnet of Bonnie Dundee.

He spurr'd to the foot of the proud Castle rock,
And with the gay Gordon he gallantly spoke:
'Let Mons Meg and her marrows speak twa words or three,
For the love of the bonnet of Bonnie Dundee.'

The Gordon demands of him which way he goes –
'Where'er shall direct me the shade of Montrose!
Your Grace in short space shall hear tidings of me,
Or that low lies the bonnet of Bonnie Dundee.'

'There are hills beyond Pentland, and lands beyond Forth,
If there's lords in the Lowlands, there's chiefs in the North;
There are wild Duniwassals, three thousand times three,   *gentlemen*
Will cry *hoigh!* for the bonnet of Bonnie Dundee.

'Away to the hills, to the caves, to the rocks –
Ere I own a usurper, I'll couch with the fox;
And tremble, false Whigs, in the midst of your glee,
You have not seen the last of my bonnet and me!'

He waved his proud hand, and the trumpets were blown,
The kettle-drums clash'd, and the horsemen rode on,
Till on Ravelston's cliffs and on Clermiston's lee,
Died away the wild war-notes of Bonnie Dundee!

Come fill up my cup, come fill up my can,
Come saddle your horses, and call up your men;
Come open the West Port and let me gang free,
And it's room for the bonnets of Bonnie Dundee!

Sir Walter Scott's verses were written in 1825, and published five years later
in The Doom of Devergoil. *Bonnie Dundee of the song is not the city of that*
name (now less than bonnie, thanks to 20th-century town planners) but the
rebel Viscount of Dundee, John Graham of Claverhouse (c.1649–89)
sometimes known as 'Bloody Clavers', who had a turbulent career opposing the
Covenanters. In 1689, after leaving the Convention, he raised an army in the
Highlands, managed to defeat the Loyalist forces at Killiecrankie on July 27,
but was mortally wounded in the hour of victory. The tune is by Charlotte
Dolby (1821–85), an English contralto whose singing impressed Mendelssohn.
He wrote the contralto part of Elijah with her in mind, dedicated the English
edition of his Six Songs *(Op. 57) to her and engaged her to sing at the Leipzig*
Gewandhaus. She composed cantatas and many songs and founded a Vocal
Academy. She married the French violinist and composer Prosper Sainton (a
professor at the Royal Academy of Music) in 1860.

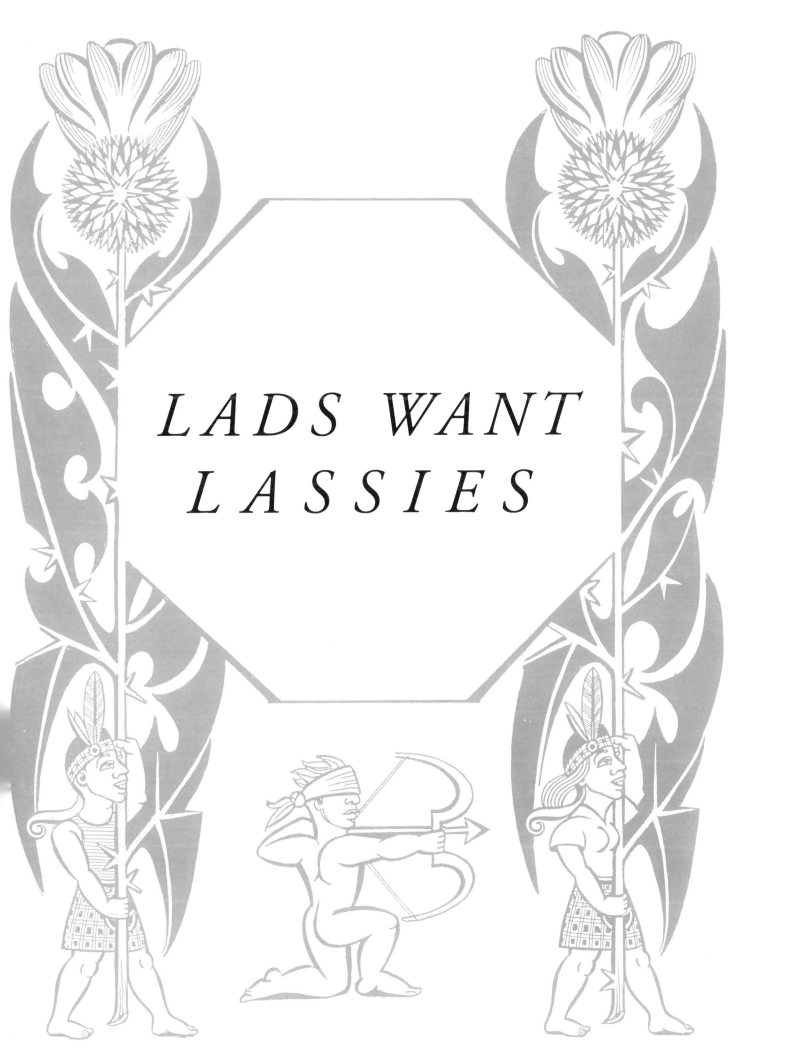

LADS WANT LASSIES

Weary Fa' You Duncan Gray ROBERT BURNS

Duncan Gray cam here to woo,
Ha, ha, the wooing o't,
On blythe Yule night when we were fu', *Christmas/drunk*
Ha, ha, the wooing o't.
Maggie coost her head fu' high,
Look'd asklent and unco skeigh' *askance/ very proud*
Gart poor Duncan stand abeigh; *aside*
Ha, ha, the wooing o't.

Duncan fleech'd, and Duncan pray'd; *wheedled*
Ha, ha, the wooing o't.
Meg was deaf as Ailsa Craig,
Ha, ha, the wooing o't.
Duncan sigh'd baith out and in,
Grat his een baith bleer't an' blin', *wept bleary/ blind*
Spak o' lowpin o'er a linn; *leaping over a waterfall*
Ha, ha, the wooing o't.

Time and Chance are but a tide,
Ha, ha, the wooing o't.
Slighted love is sair to bide, *hard to endure*
Ha, ha, the wooing o't.
Shall I like a fool quoth he,
For a haughty hizzie die? *hussy*
She may gae to – France for me!
Ha, ha, the wooing o't.

How it comes let Doctors tell,
Ha, ha, the wooing o't.
Meg grew sick as he grew heal, *well*
Ha, ha, the wooing o't.
Something in her bosom wrings,
For relief a sigh she brings;
And O her een, they spak sic things!
Ha, ha, the wooing o't.

Duncan was a lad o' grace,
Ha, ha, the wooing o't.
Maggie's was a piteous case,
Ha, ha, the wooing o't.
Duncan could na be her death,
Swelling pity smoor'd his Wrath; *smothered*
Now they're crouse and canty baith, *merry/ cheerful*
Ha, ha, the wooing o't.

When Burns sent this delightful song of love, courtship and marriage to the publisher George Thomson in 1792, he wrote: 'Duncan Gray is that kind of light-horse gallop of an old air which precludes sentiment. The ludicrous is the leading feature.' The poet comes close to Shakespeare in this song as in many of his other comic love songs. Its inspiration came (as did his earlier bawdy version, 'Weary fa' you Duncan Gray') from a traditional song in the Herd collection: 'Duncan he came here to woo / On a day when we were fou,/ And Meg she swore that she wou'd spew,/ If he gaed her the girdin o't.' The tune is in the Caledonian Pocket Companion *but Burns believed it had been composed by a carman in Glasgow. This version is from the* Scots Musical Museum *(vol. II, no. 160). 'Lammas', 1 August, is one of the 4 Scottish 'quarter' days, which divide up the year for administrative purposes. The others are Martinmas, 11 November; Candlemas, 2 February; and Whitsunday, 15 May. ' Mess John' is a light-hearted name for a (usually Presbyterian) minister, or for ministers in general.*

Weary fa' you Duncan Gray, *befall*
Ha, ha the girdin o't, *girthing (copulating)*
Wae gae by you, Duncan Gray,
Ha, ha, the girdin o't:
When a' the lave gae to their play,
Then I maun sit the lee lang day
And jeeg the cradle wi' my knee,
And a' for the girdin o't.

Bonnie was the Lammas moon,
Ha, ha, the girdin' o't;
Glowrin a' the hills aboon, *gleaming/ above*
Ha, ha, the girdin o't;
The girdin brak, the beast cam down,
I tint my curch and baith my shoon, *lost/ cap*
And Duncan, ye're an unco loun *a strange fellow*
Wae on the bad girdin o't.

But Duncan, gin ye'll keep your aith, *oath*
Ha, ha, the girdin o't,
I'se bless you wi' my hindmost breath
Ha, ha, the girdin o't;
Duncan, gin ye'll keep your aith,
The beast again can bear us baith.
And auld Mess John will mend the skaith *hurt*
And clout the bad girdin o't. *patch*

20 HO RO, MO NIGHEAN DONN BHOIDHEACH *GAELIC*

Brightly

Ho rò, mo nighean donn bhòidh - each, Hi rì, mo nighean donn bhòidh - each, Mo

chai - leag lagh - ach, bhòidh - each, Cha phò - sainn ach thu. A

Phei - gi dhonn nam blàth - shùl, Gur trom a thug mi gràdh dhuit: Tha

t'iomh - aigh ghaoil, 'us t'àill - eachd A ghnàth tigh'nn fo m'ùidh.

con Ped.

CHORUS AFTER EACH VERSE

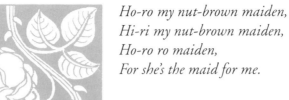
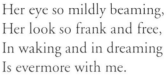

Ho rò, mo nighean donn bhòidheach,
Hi rì, mo nighean donn bhòidheach,
Mo chaileag laghach, bhòidheach,
Cha phòsainn ach thu.

Ho-ro my nut-brown maiden,
Hi-ri my nut-brown maiden,
Ho-ro ro maiden,
For she's the maid for me.

A Pheigi dhonn nam blàthshùl,
Gur trom a thug mi gràdh dhuit:
Tha t'ìomhaigh ghaoil, 'us t'àilleachd
A ghnàth tigh'nn fo m'ùidh.

Her eye so mildly beaming,
Her look so frank and free,
In waking and in dreaming
Is evermore with me.

Cha cheil mi air an t-saoghal
Gu bheil mo mhiann's mo ghaol ort;
'S ged chaidh mi uait air faondradh,
Cha chaochail mo rùn.

O Mary, mild-eyed Mary,
By land, or on the sea,
Though time and tide may vary,
My heart beats true to thee.

'Nuair bha mi ann ad làthair,
Bu shona bha mo làithean –
A' sealbhachadh do mhànrain,
'Us àille do ghnùis.

And since from thee I parted,
A long and weary while,
I wander heavy-hearted
With longing for thy smile.

Gnùis aoidheil, bhanail, mhàlda
Na h-òigh a's caoimhe nàdur;
I suairce, ceanail, bàigheil,
Làn gràis agus mùirn.

In Glasgow and Dunedin
Were maidens fair to see,
But never a Lowland maiden
Could lure mine eyes from thee.

Ach riamh o'n dh'fhàg mi t'fhianuis,
Gu bheil mi dubhach, cianail;
Mo chridhe trom 'ga phianadh
Le iarguin do rùin.

Mine eyes that never vary
From pointing to the glen
Where blooms my Highland Mary
Like wild-rose 'neath the Ben.

Ge lurach air a' chabhsair
Na mnathan òga Gallda,
A rìgh! gur beag mo gheall-s'
Air bhi sealltainn 'nan gnùis.

And when with blossoms laden
Bright summer comes again,
I'll fetch my nut-brown maiden
Down from the bonnie glen.

'S ann tha mo rùn 's na beanntaibh,
Far bheil mo rìbhinn ghreannar,
Mar ròs am fàsach Shamhraidh,
An gleann fad' o shùil.

This old favourite was translated from the Gaelic by Professor John Stuart
Blackie (1809–95), a banker's son who was born in Glasgow and educated
in Aberdeen, Edinburgh, Göttingen and Berlin. Blackie studied theology
and law, but practised neither discipline although he was called to the Bar in
1834. (He published a metrical translation of Goethe's Faust *the same year).*
Later he became Professor of Humanities (Latin) at Aberdeen University and
then Professor of Greek at Edinburgh. He was a fervent Scottish Nationalist
and great advocate of Celtic culture. He led the campaign to found and
endow the Chair of Celtic at Edinburgh in 1882.

Ach 'n uair a thig an Samhradh,
Bheir mise sgrìob do'n ghleann ud,
'S gu'n toir mi leam do'n Ghalldachd,
Gu h-annsail, am flùr.

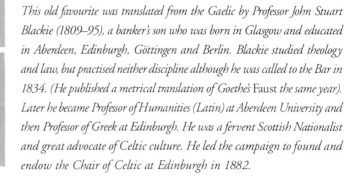

Moderate

Let us haste to Kel - vin Grove,— bon - nie las - sie, O! Through its

ma - zes let us rove, bon - nie las - sie, O. Where the ro - ses in their pride Deck the

bon - nie din - gle side, Where the mid - night fai - ries glide,— bon - nie las - sie, O!

con Ped.

Let us haste to Kelvin Grove, bonnie lassie, O!
Through its mazes let us rove, bonnie lassie, O.
Where the roses in their pride
Deck the bonnie dingle side,
Where the midnight fairies glide, bonnie lassie, O!

Let us wander by the mill, bonnie lassie, O!
To the cove beside the rill, bonnie lassie, O!
Where the glens rebound the call
Of the roaring waters' fall,
Through the mountain's rocky hall,
      bonnie lassie, O!

O Kelvin banks are fair, bonnie lassie, O!
When the summer we are there, bonnie lassie, O!
There the May-pink's crimson plume
Throws a soft but sweet perfume,
Round the yellow banks o' broom,
      bonnie lassie, O!

Though I dare not call thee mine, bonnie lassie, O,
As the smile of fortune's thine, bonnie lassie, O,
Yet with fortune on my side,
I could stay thy father's pride,
And win thee for my bride, bonnie lassie, O.

But the frowns of fortune lour, bonnie lassie, O.
On thy lover at this hour, bonnie lassie, O,
Ere yon golden orb of day
Wake the warblers on the spray,
From this land I must away, bonnie lassie, O.

Then farewell to Kelvin Grove, bonnie lassie, O!
And adieu to all I love, bonnie lassie, O,
To the river winding clear,
To the fragrant scented brier,
Even to thee of all most dear, bonnie lassie, O!

When upon a foreign shore, bonnie lassie, O,
Should I fall midst battle's roar, bonnie lassie, O,
Then Helen, shouldst thou hear
Of thy lover on his bier,
To his memory shed a tear, bonnie lassie, O.

Kelvingrove on the river Kelvin, near where it joins the River Clyde, is now part of the City of Glasgow. The late 19th-century Kelvingrove Art Gallery and Museum is in Kelvingrove Park opposite the University, and both park and gallery are popular meeting, or gathering, places for Glaswegians. This tune appears in Smith's Scottish Minstrel *(vol. II, 1824) as 'Kelvin Water', but it was long known as 'O the shearin's no for you' which was the first line of the old song.*

I the rich— re - ward se-cure – The love-ly Ma - ry Mor - i-son.

O Mary, at thy window be,
It is the wish'd, the trysted hour!
Those smiles and glances let me see,
That make the miser's treasure poor.
How blithely wad I bide the stoure,   *endure/ struggle*
A weary slave frae sun to sun;
Could I the rich reward secure –
The lovely Mary Morison.

Yestreen when to the trembling string
The dance gaed through the lighted ha',
To thee my fancy took its wing,
I sat, but neither heard nor saw:
Though this was fair and that was braw,
And yon the toast of a' the town,
I sigh'd, and said amang them a',
'Ye are na Mary Morison.'

O Mary, canst thou wreck his peace,
Wha for thy sake wad gladly die!
Or canst thou break that heart of his,
Whase only faut is loving thee!
If love for love thou wilt na gie,
At least be pity to me shown;
A thought ungentle canna be
The thought o' Mary Morison.

This song is generally agreed to be one of Burns's finest lyrics, but he himself was rather disparaging of it in his later years: 'The song is one of my juvenile works', he wrote to the publisher George Thomson, in March, 1792, '– I leave it among your hands. I do not think it very remarkable, either for its merits or demerits. – It is impossible, at least I feel it in my stinted powers, to be always original, entertaining and witty.' Who Mary Morison was, is a matter for some debate. Burns set his verses to the tune 'Duncan Davison' (below) but it is better known sung to 'The Miller', given here.

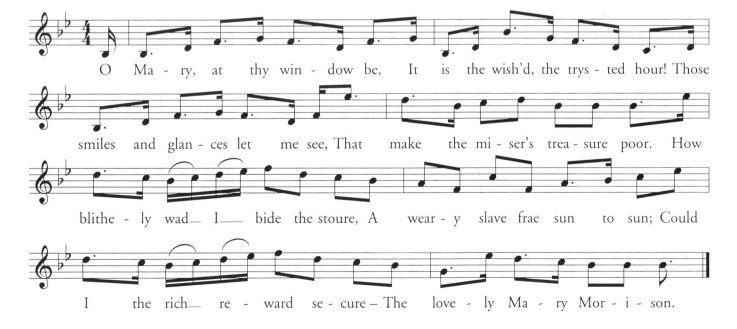

O Ma - ry, at thy win - dow be, It is the wish'd, the trys - ted hour! Those

smiles and glan - ces let me see, That make the mi - ser's trea - sure poor. How

blithe - ly wad— I— bide the stoure, A wear - y slave frae sun to sun; Could

I the rich— re - ward se - cure – The love - ly Ma - ry Mor - i - son.

Moderate

con Ped.

Thy cheek is o'— the— ro-se's hue, My on-ly joe— and— dear-ie, O, Thy

neck is like— the— sil-ler dew, Up-on the bank— sae brier-ie, O; Thy

teeth are o' the i-vo-ry, O sweet's the twink-le— o' thine e'e, Nae

joy nae plea-sure— blinks on me, My on-ly joe— and— dear-ie O.

Thy cheek is o' the rose's hue,
My only joe and dearie, O,   *sweetheart*
Thy neck is like the siller dew,
Upon the bank sae brierie, O;
Thy teeth are o' the ivory,
O sweet's the twinkle o' thine e'e,
Nae joy nae pleasure blinks on me,
My only joe and dearie O.

The birdie sings upon the thorn
Its sang o' joy fu' cheerie, O!
Rejoicing in the simmer morn,
Nae care to mak' it eerie, O! *melancholy*
But little kens the sangster sweet
Aught o' the care I hae to meet,
That gars my restless bosom beat,
My only joe and dearie, O!

When we were bairnies on yon brae,
And youth was blinkin' bonny O,
Aft we wad daff the leelang day , *act playfully*
Our joys fu' sweet and monie O.
Aft I wad chace thee o'er the lee,
And round about the thornie tree,
Or pu' the wild flowers a' for thee,
My only joe and dearie, O!

I ha'e a wish I canna tine *can't get rid of*
'Mang a' the cares that grieve me O!
A wish that thou wert ever mine,
And never mair to leave me O.
Then I wad daut thee night and day, *fondle*
Nae ither war'ly care wad ha'e *worldly*
Till life's warm stream forgot to play,
My only joe and dearie, O.

These verses were written at the request of an Edinburgh publisher, Mr Oliver, who had heard the tune sung at the Harlequin Highlander's pantomime at the Circus. Richard Gall trained as a joiner but later joined Ramsay's Edinburgh printing office and he died in 1801, when he was only in his 25th year. This song appeared posthumously in 1803, in the final volume of the Scots Musical Museum *(no. 531).*

AY, WAUKIN, O

Fairly slow

Ay, wau - kin, O, Wau - kin still and wea - rie! Sleep I can get nane For

think - ing on my dea - rie. Sim - mer's a plea - sant time: Flowers of ev' - ry co - lour; The

wa - ter rins o'er the heugh, And I long for my true lo - ver.

con Ped.

Fine

D.C.

CHORUS AFTER EVERY VERSE

Ay, waukin, O, always awake
Waukin still and wearie!
Sleep I can get nane
For thinking on my dearie.

Simmer's a pleasant time:
Flowers of ev'ry colour;
The water rins o'er the heugh, bank
And I long for my true lover.

When I sleep I dream,
When I wauk I'm irie; apprehensive
Sleep I can get nane
For thinking on my dearie.

Lanely night comes on,
A' the lave are sleepin: rest
I think on my bonny lad
And I bleer my een wi' greetin.

Ay, waukin, O,
Waukin still and wearie!
Sleep I can get nane
For thinking on my dearie.

'I invariably hold it sacrilege to add anything of my own to help out with the shatter'd wrecks of these venerable old compositions . . .' wrote Burns to William Tytler in August 1787, but the poet has been criticized for over-pruning and over-refining some artless originals to produce spiritless drawing-room pieces. For this one however, he expanded a fragment from Herd's manuscripts and the result is a touching little love song of universality and absolute simplicity. The tune probably dates from the 17th century. There are two versions in the Scots Musical Museum, *(vol. III, no. 213 and vol. IV, no. 382) and this setting comes from Napier's* Scots Songs *(vol. I, no. 61) which was published in 1790, the same year as vol. III of the* Museum.

Wilt thou be my dear - ie? When sor - row wrings— thy— gen - tle heart,— O,—

wilt thou let me chear thee? By the trea - sure of my soul – That's the love I— bear thee – I—

swear and vow,— that on - ly thou Shall— ev - er be my dear - ie.

On - ly thou, I— swear and vow— Shall— ev - er be my dear - ie.

Wilt thou be my dearie?
When sorrow wrings thy gentle heart,
O, wilt thou let me chear thee?
By the treasure of my soul –
That's the love I bear thee –
I swear and vow, that only thou
Shall ever be my dearie.
Only thou, I swear and vow
Shall ever be my dearie.

Lassie, say thou lo'es me;
Or if thou wilt na be my ain,
Say na thou'lt refuse me:
If it winna, canna be,
Thou for thine may chuse me,
Let me, Lassie, quickly die,
Trusting that thou lo'es me.
Lassie, let me quickly die,
Trusting that thou lo'es me.

This song was written for Miss Janet Miller of Dalswinton, and the poet refers to it in a letter (March 3, 1794) to Alexander Cunningham: 'Apropos, do you know the much admired Highland air called The sutor's dochter? It is a firstrate favourite of mine, and I have written what I reckon one of my best songs to it. I will send it to you, set as I think it should be, and as it was sung with great applause in many fashionable groups by Major Robertson, of Lude, who was here with his corps.' The air is found in Stewart's Reels, *1763 and in McGlashan's* Strathspey Reels, *1780. A 'sutor' is a shoemaker or cobbler.*

CHORUS AFTER EACH VERSE

Ca' the yowes to the knowes,   ewes/ knolls
Ca' them whare the heather grows,
Ca' them whare the burnie rowes,   stream runs
My bonnie dearie.

As I gaed down the water-side,
There I met my shepherd-lad,
He row'd me sweetly in his plaid,   wrapped
And he ca'd me his dearie.

Will ye gang down the water-side
And see the waves sae sweetly glide
Beneath the hazels spreading wide,
The moon it shines fu' clearly.

I was bred up at nae sic school,
My shepherd-lad, to play the fool,
And a' the day to sit in dool,   misery
And nae body to see me.

Ye shall get gowns and ribbons meet,
Cauf-leather shoon upon your feet,
And in my arms ye'se lie and sleep,
And ye sall be my dearie.

If ye'll but stand to what ye've said,
I'se gang wi' you, my shepherd-lad,
And ye may rowe me in your plaid,
And I sall be your dearie.

While waters wimple to the sea;   meander
While day blinks in the lift sae hie,   shines in the sky
Till clay-cauld death sall blin' my e'e
Ye sall be my dearie.

Burns sent this song to James Johnson for inclusion in the Scots Musical Museum *of 1790 (vol. III, no. 264). 'This beautiful song is in the true old Scotch taste', he wrote, 'and I do not know that ever either air or words, were in print before'. He recast the original, expanding the first stanza into two, making various other changes and adding a final stanza of his own. A few years later he sent a completely different version (only the chorus remained the same) to the publisher*

George Thomson: 'I am flattered at your adopting "Ca the yowes to the knowes," as it was owing to me that it ever saw the light. – About seven years ago, I was well acquainted with a worthy little fellow of a Clergyman, a Mr Clunzie, who sang it charmingly; and at my request, Mr Clarke took it down from his singing.' Stephen Clarke was an Edinburgh organist and chief musical advisor to Burns in the Scots Musical Museum *venture. The new song appeared in Thomson's* Original Scotch Airs *in 1805: the lovers' dialogue and the ballad touches of the first setting had gone, to be replaced by 'a pre–Romantic landscape of waves, ruined towers, and fairies dancing in the moonlight, to which is added an impression of protective tenderness suggested by the melody itself.'*

Ca' the yowes to the knowes,
Ca' them whare the heather grows,
Ca' them whare the burnie rowes,
My bonnie Dearie.

Hark, the mavis' evening sang   song-thrush
Sounding Clouden's woods amang;
Then a faulding let us gang,   enclosing (animals)
My bonnie Dearie.

We'll gae down by Clouden side,
Through the hazels spreading wide
O'er the waves, that sweetly glide
To the moon sae clearly.

Yonder Clouden's silent towers,
Where at moonshine midnight hours
O'er the dewy bending flowers
Fairies dance sae cheary.

Ghaist nor bogle shalt thou fear;   ghost/ hobgoblin
Thou'rt to Love and Heaven sae dear,
Nocht of Ill may come thee near,   nothing
My bonnie Dearie.

Fair and lovely as thou art,
Thou hast stown my very heart;   stolen
I can die – but canna part,
My bonnie Dearie.

TURN YE TO ME *by John Wilson (Christopher North)*

Moderate

con Ped.

The stars are shin-ing cheer-i-ly, cheer-i-ly, Ho - ro Mhai-ri dhu, turn ye to me; The

sea-mew is moan-ing drear-i-ly, drear-i-ly, Ho - ro Mhai-ri dhu, turn ye to me!

Cold is the storm wind that ruf-fles his breast, But warm are the down-y plumes lin-ing his nest. Cold

blows— the storm— there, soft falls the snow,—then Ho - ro Mhair-i dhu, turn ye to me!

The stars are shining cheerily, cheerily,
Horo Mhairi dhu, turn ye to me;
The sea-mew is moaning drearily, drearily,   *seagull*
Horo Mhairi dhu, turn ye to me!
Cold is the storm wind that ruffles his breast,
But warm are the downy plumes lining his nest.
Cold blows the storm there, soft falls the snow, then
Horo Mhairi dhu, turn ye to me!

The waves are dancing, merrily, merrily,
Horo Mhairi dhu, turn ye to me.
The sea birds are wailing, wearily, wearily,
Horo Mhairi dhu, turn ye to me.
Hushed be thy moaning, lone bird of the sea,
Thy home on the rocks is a shelter to thee;
Thy house is the angry wave, mine but the lonely grave,
Horo Mhairi dhu, turn ye to me.

'Turn Ye to Me' is one of the most enduringly popular of Hebridean songs. The melody was taken down from the singing of Misses Anne and Janet McLeod of Gesto in Skye and was first published in Alexander Campbell's Albyn's Anthology *of 1816. Christopher North was the pseudonym of John Wilson (1785–1854), son of a wealthy gauze manufacturer in Paisley who was educated at Glasgow University and Magdalen College, Oxford. Wilson used his inheritance to buy an estate in the Lake District where he became a close friend of Wordsworth, Coleridge and de Quincey. He published poetry and prose, later trained as an advocate, and in 1817 helped to establish Blackwood's Magazine, for which he published many notable series, including 'Noctes Ambrosianae'. For political reasons and despite his lack of formal qualifications, he was appointed Professor of Moral Philosophy at Edinburgh University, a post he held for over thirty years, relying on a friend to supply his lecture notes.*

Air feasgar ciùin Cèitein 's mi teurnadh an t-slèibhe,
Hug òro is eutrom mo cheum air làr;
A' ghrian anns na speuran a' dèarrsadh gu ceutach,
Is eunlaidh nan geugan a' seinn an dàn;
Tha'n t-allt ruith don abhainn le caithream s le ceòl;
Na craobhan fo'n duilleach s na lusan nan glòir;
Na beanntan s na gleanntan nam maise ro òirdheirc'
Is thall air a' chòmhnard tha òigh mo ghràidh.

A chailin gun fhoill, bidh mo dhùrachd a chaoidh dhuit,
A mhaighdeann ghlan aoidheil is caoimhe sùil;
Tha grinneas do dhòighean fa m'chomhair an còmhnuidh
Is fòs do bhinn chòmhradh tha mòdhar ciùin;
Is duilich leam fhèin mar d'èirich dhomh àgh,
S gur suarach mo bhuannachd s nach buanaich i là,
Na'm biodh agam saibhreas sin thoillinn uait fàbhar
Is rachainn gun athadh nad dhàil a nunn.

Is truagh nach do stiùir thu, a Fhreasdail, mo chùrsa
Nad chaoimhneas d'a h-ionnsuidh an tùs mo rè;
Sin bhithinn-sa eudmhor, deanadach, gleusda
An àite bhi gèilleachd roimh cheann na rèis.
Roimh'n am so b'e dòchas bu dhòmhsa mar mhaoin;
Bhiodh doilgheas an la-'n-diugh am màireach air sgaoil;
Ach thàinig thu, Mhòrag, is leòn thu le gaol mi
Nach tarruing gu faochadh mur taobh thu rium fèin.

Tha 'm feasgar a'ciaradh o'n theirig a'ghrian;
Tha rionnag san iarmailt os cionn an dùin;
Eòin bhuchainn a'bharraich air casgadh an caithreim:
C'ar son tha mi fanachd aig taobh a' chùirn?
Sud thall air an rèidhlean gun duin' ach i fèin
A' mhaighdeann fhìor-uasal nam buadh is nam beus:
A dheòin no a dh'aindeoin, gur daingeann mo spèis di,
S air Nàile! gu'n tèid mi 'na dàil a nunn.

THE BIRKS OF ABERFELDY *ROBERT BURNS*

Bon - nie las - sie, will ye go, ___ Will ye go, ___ will ye go, ___

Bon - nie las - sie, will ye go To the birks of A - ber - fel - dy? Now

sim - mer blinks on flow - 'ry braes, And o'er the crys - tal stream - lets ___ plays; Come,

let us spend the light - some days In the birks of A - ber - fel - dy.

CHORUS AFTER EVERY VERSE

Bonnie lassie, will ye go,
Will ye go, will ye go,
Bonnie lassie, will ye go
To the birks of Aberfeldy?   birches

Now simmer blinks on flow'ry braes,   *summer gleams*
And o'er the crystal streamlets plays;
Come, let us spend the lightsome days
In the birks of Aberfeldy.

The little birdies blythely sing,
While o'er their heads the hazels hing;
Or lightly flit on wanton wing
In the birks of Aberfeldy.

The braes ascend like lofty wa's,
The foamy stream deep-roaring fa's,
O'er hung wi' fragrant-spreading shaws,   *woods*
The birks of Aberfeldy. –

The hoary cliffs are crown'd wi' flowers,
White o'er the linns the burnie pours,   *waterfalls*
And rising weets wi' misty showers   *wets*
The birks of Aberfeldy.

Let Fortune's gifts at random flee,
They ne'er shall draw a wish frae me;
Supremely blest wi' love and thee
In the birks of Aberfeldy.

This song (Scots Musical Museum, vol. II, no. 113) was inspired by Burns's first Highland tour in the company of William Nichol, of Edinburgh High School: 'I composed these stanzas', he wrote, 'standing under the falls of Aberfeldy, at or near Moness'. The catchy melody dates back to a manuscript of 1694 and the chorus was based on the older, less polite folksong, 'The Birks of Abergeldie'. Burns has been criticized in this instance for replacing 'a simple artless original' with 'an effete and spiritless drawing-room piece', but 'The birks of Aberfeldy' remains one of his most popular songs. (Calamanco is a glossy woollen fabric woven with a checked design that shows on one side only).

Bonny lassie, will ye go,
Will ye go, will ye go
Bonny lassie, will ye go
To the birks o' Abergeldie?

Ye shall get a gown of silk,
A gown of silk, a gown of silk,
Ye shall get a gown of silk,
And coat of calinmancoe.

Na, kind Sir, I dare nae gang,
I dare nae gang, I dare nae gang.
Na, kind Sir, I dare nae gang,
My minnie she'll be angry:

Sair, fair wad she flyte,
Wad she flyte, wad she flyte,
Sair, fair wad she flyte,
And fair wad she ban me.

Brightly

con Ped.

Whar hae ye been a'— day, My— boy— Tam-my? Whar hae ye been a'— day,

My— boy— Tam-my? I've been by burn and flo-w'ry brae, Mea-dow green and moun-tain grey,

Cour-tin o' this young thing, Just come frae her Mam-my.

Whar hae ye been a' day,
My boy Tammy?
Whar hae ye been a' day,
My boy Tammy?
I've been by burn and flow'ry brae,
Meadow green and mountain grey,
Courtin o' this young thing,
Just come frae her Mammy.

And whar gat ye that young thing,
My boy Tammy?
And whar gat ye that young thing,
My boy Tammy?
I got her down in yonder how,   *hollow*
Smiling on a broomy know,   *knoll*
Herding ae wee Lamb and Ewe,
For her poor Mammy.

What said ye to the bonny bairn,
My boy Tammy?
What said ye to the bonny bairn,
My boy Tammy?
I prais'd her een sae lovely blue,
Her dimpled cheek, and cherry mou;
I pree'd it aft; as ye may true –   *kissed / believe*
She said she'd tell her Mammy.

I held her to my beating heart,
My young, my smiling lammie!
I held her to my beatin' heart,
My young, my smiling lammie!
I hae a house, it cost me dear,
I've walth o' plenishan' and geer;   *riches*
Ye'se get it a', war't ten times mair,
Gin ye will leave your Mammy.

The smile gaed aff her bonnie face –
I manna leave my Mammy.
The smile gaed aff her bonnie face –
I manna leave my Mammy.
She's ge'en me meat, she's ge'en me claise,
She's been my comfort a' my days –
My Father's death brought mony waes!
I canna leave my Mammy.

We'll tak her hame and mak her fain,   *glad*
My ain kind-hearted Lammy.
We'll tak her hame and mak her fain,
My ain kind-hearted Lammy.
We'll gee her meat, we'll gee her claise,
We'll be her comfort a' her days.
The wee thing gi'es her hand, and says,
There! gang and ask my Mammy.

Has she been to Kirk wi' thee,
My boy Tammy?
She been to kirk wi' thee
My boy Tammy?
She has been to kirk wi' me,
And the tear was in her ee –
But O! she's but a young thing,
Just come frae her Mammy!

Hector Macneil was born near Roslin in 1746. He displayed early literary talent but circumstances took him to the West Indies where he spent many years as a negro-driver (he was a strenuous champion of slavery and wrote a pamphlet in its defence). He was over forty, penniless and in poor health when he returned to Scotland to devote himself to writing (poetry and prose) and although he was editor of The Scots Magazine *for a time he was never successful financially and in 1818 died without leaving the where-withal for his funeral expenses. Like Burns and Lady Nairne, Macneil took traditional fragments of songs and ballads and expanded them to fit existing tunes, in this case the old song: Is she fit to soop the house, my boy Tammie?/ Is she fit to soop the house, my boy Tammie?/ She's just as fit to soop the house as the cat to tak' a mouse;/ And yet she's but a young thing, just come frae her mammie.// 'My boy Tammy' first appeared in 1791 in an Edinburgh magazine called* The Bee *then, with the melody, in Napier's* Collection, *vol. II, 1792 and the* Scots Musical Museum *of 1803 (vol. VI, no. 502). The tune is similar to that of 'Muirland Willie' from Thomson's* Orpheus Caledonius *of 1733 (vol. I, no. 27).*

CHORUS AFTER EACH VERSE

Lang hae we parted been,
Lassie, my dearie;
Now we are met again,
Lassie, lie near me!

Near me, near me,
Lassie, lie near me,
Lang hast thou lien thy lane,   lain alone
Lassie, lie near me.

A' that I hae endured,
Lassie, my dearie,
Here in thy arms is cur'd,
Lassie, lie near me.

Burns made two settings of the traditional tune 'Laddie lie near me' but
he withdrew the second one, 'Twas na her bonnie blue e'e was my ruin',
from his publisher George Thomson, writing to him that 'it was neither
worthy of my name, nor of your book'. For this one, which is no. 218, vol.
III of the Scots Musical Museum *(1790), Burns took traditional*
material and added a second verse to the existing verse and chorus.

BONNIE CHARLIE
(MOSTLY)

THERE'LL NEVER BE PEACE TILL JAMIE COMES HAME

Moderately slow

By— yon cas - tle wa' at the close— of the— day, I—

heard a man— sing, tho' his head it was— grey, And—

as he was— sing - ing, the tears— doon came, 'There'll—

nev - er— be peace— till Ja - mie comes— hame.'

By yon castle wa' at the close of the day,
I heard a man sing, tho' his head it was grey,
And as he was singing, the tears doon came,
'There'll never be peace till Jamie comes hame.'

The Church is in ruins, the State is in jars,
Delusions, oppressions, and murderous wars,
We dare na weel say't, but we ken wha's to blame,
'There'll never be peace till Jamie comes hame.'

My seven braw sons for Jamie drew sword,
And now I greet round their green beds in the yerd;
It brak the sweet heart of my faithfu' auld Dame,
'There'll never be peace till Jamie comes hame.'

Now, life is a burden that bows me down,
Sin I tint my bairns, and he tint his crown;   *lost*
But till my last moments my words are the same,
'There'll never be peace till Jamie comes hame.'

It seems logical to begin this section with a song about Charles Edward Stewart's father, or grandfather. His grandfather was of course King James VII of Scotland, and the fourth Stewart to rule all Britain. James's conversion to the Catholic faith was tolerated by his subjects until he tried to make toleration for everyone a law of the land; so Episcopalians and Presbyterians (who had hitherto fought against each other) united to drive him into exile and put a Dutch Calvinist on the British throne. The man who complains that 'The church is in ruins' may be an Episcopalian who hates having a Dutch Presbyterian for king, or a Presbyterian who hates the kingship of George Hanover, the German Episcopalian who came after. In the latter case 'Jamie' is most likely to be the 8th James Stewart whose efforts to gain the crown in 1715 were easily crushed by the Duke of Argyll. This Jamie – called 'The Old Pretender' by his enemies – was father of Charles Edward Stewart, 'The Young Pretender'. 'You must know a beautiful Jacobite air', wrote Burns to his friend Alexander Cunningham in March 1791, '"There'll never be peace till Jamie comes hame."– When Political combustion ceases to be the object of Princes and Patriots, it then you know, becomes the lawful prey of Historians and Poets . . . If you like the air, and if the stanzas hit your fancy, you cannot imagine, my dear Friend, how much you would oblige me if by the charms of your delightful voice you would give my honest effusion to "The memory of joys that are past," to the few friends whom you indulge in that pleasure.' Strangely enough, Hogg in his Jacobite Reliques, Series II (1821) *refers to this as 'an old song without any alterations'. Burns noted that the tune was sometimes called 'There's few gude fellows when Jamie's awa'. It appears in* The Caledonian Pocket Companion *(1743).*

Where hae ye been a' the day,
Bonnie laddie, Highland laddie?
Saw ye him that's far away,
Bonnie laddie, Highland laddie?
On his head a bonnet blue,
Bonnie laddie, Highland laddie,
Tartan plaid and tartan trew,
Bonnie laddie, Highland laddie!

When he drew his gude braid sword,
Bonnie laddie, Highland laddie,
Then he gave his royal word,
Bonnie laddie, Highland laddie,
That frae the field he'd never flee,
Bonnie laddie, Highland laddie;
But wi' his friends would live or dee,
Bonnie laddie, Highland laddie.

Weary fa the Lawland loon,
Bonnie laddie, Highland laddie,
Wha took frae him the British crown,
Bonnie laddie, Highland laddie;
But blessings on the kilted clans,
Bonnie laddie, Highland laddie,
That fought for him at Prestonpans,
Bonnie laddie, Highland laddie.

Among several versions sung to this catchy tune is the well-known Canadian sea shanty Donkey-Riding *('Were you ever in Quebec, donkey-riding, donkey-riding?'). Possibly it was picked up by Canadian sailors visiting Scottish ports in the last century. Prince Charles's victory at Prestonpans (21 September 1745) is also celebrated in the popular song 'Johnnie Cope' (see pages 8–9.) The second version of 'Highland laddie' is typical of many Jacobite songs which cunningly mix love and loyalty to the chevalier.*

If thou'lt play me fair play,
Bonnie Laddie, Highland laddie,
Another year for thee I'll stay,
Bonnie laddie, Highland laddie;
For a' the lasses here abouts,
Bonnie laddie, Highland laddie;
Marry none but Geordie's louts,
Bonnie laddie, Highland laddie.

The time shall come when their bad choice,
Bonnie laddie, Highland laddie,
They will repent, and we rejoice,
Bonnie laddie, Highland laddie;
I'd take thee in thy Highland trews,
Bonnie laddie, Highland laddie,
Before the rogues that wear the blues,
Bonnie laddie, Highland laddie.

Our torments from no cause do spring,
Bonnie lassie, Lowland lassie,
But fighting for our lawful king,
Bonnie lassie, Lowland lassie;
Our king's reward will come in time,
Bonnie lassie, Lowland lassie;
And constant Jenny shall be mine,
Bonnie lassie, Lowland lassie.

There's no distress that earth can bring,
Bonnie lassie, Lowland lassie,
But I'd endure for our true king,
Bonnie lassie, Lowland lassie;
And were my Jenny but my own,
Bonnie lassie, Lowland lassie,
I'd undervalue Geordie's crown,
Bonnie lassie, Lowland lassie.

Come o'er the stream, Char - lie, dear Char - lie, brave Char - lie, Come o'er the stream,

Char - lie, and dine wi' Mac - Lean; And though you be wea - ry, we'll make your heart

chee - ry, And wel - come our Char - lie and his ro - yal train. We'll

bring down the red deer, we'll bring down the black steer, The lamb from the

brack - an, and doe from the glen; The salt sea we'll har - ry, and

bring to our Char - lie, The cream from the bo - thy, and curd from the pan.

CHORUS AFTER EVERY VERSE

Come o'er the stream, Charlie, dear Charlie, dear Charlie,
Come o'er the stream, Charlie, and dine wi' MacLean;
And though you be weary, we'll make your heart cheery,
And welcome our Charlie and his royal train.

We'll bring down the red deer,
                                    we'll bring down the black steer,
The lamb from the brackan, and doe from the glen;
The salt sea we'll harry, and bring to our Charlie,
The cream from the bothy, and curd from the pan.

And you shall drink freely the dews o' Glen Sheerly,
That stream in the starlight where kings dinna ken;
And deep be your meed of the wine that is red,
To drink to your sire and his friend the MacLean.

If ought will invite you, or more will delight you,
'Tis ready – a troop of our bold Highlandmen
Shall range on the heather, with bonnet and feather,
Strong arms and broad claymores, three hundred and ten.

James Hogg included this song in his Jacobite Reliques, Series II. *The air is a Highland one and the verses a free translation from the Gaelic. Hogg did a nice line in 'Jacobite' songs referring to the rebellions of 1715 and 1745, usually with an eye to commerce: 'If you therefore adopt the songs, please publish them simply as Jacobite songs,' he wrote to publisher George Thomson, 'leaving the world to find out whether they are old or new. This has a far better effect than saying "A Jacobite song by such and such an author." The very idea that perhaps they may be of a former day and written by some sennachie of the clan gives them double interest.' Hogg, or the Ettrick Shepherd as he was more familiarly known, was born on Ettrickhall Farm in Selkirkshire in 1770. He tended sheep as a boy and only had a spasmodic education but he persevered in his writing and Sir Walter Scott, then Sheriff of Selkirkshire, encouraged him. His most remarkable work is the macabre novel* Confessions of a Justified Sinner *but he wrote a large number of works in both verse and prose.*

Oh, Char - lie is my darl - ing, My darl - ing, my darl - ing; Char - lie is my darl - ing, The young Chev - a - lier. 'Twas on a Mon - day morn - ing, Right ear - ly in the year, When Char - lie came to our— toun, The— young Chev - a - lier.

REPEAT CHORUS AFTER EACH VERSE

Oh, Charlie is my darling,
My darling, my darling;
Charlie is my darling,
The young Chevalier.

'Twas on a Monday morning,
Right early in the year,
When Charlie came to our toun,
The young Chevalier.

Both Burns and Lady Nairne were staunch Jacobites – Lady Nairne's family having been closely involved in the rebellion of 1745. Burns's version of an old ballad about Bonnie Prince Charlie retains its amorous elements. The more puritanical Carolina Nairne's version keeps strictly loyal to the Jacobite cause. Of the two probably Lady Nairne's is now better known. The tune to which hers is sung differs slightly from that of Burns's contribution to the Scots Musical Museum *of 1796 (vol. V, no. 428).*

As he came marching up the street,
The pipes play'd loud and clear,
And a' the folk came running out
To meet the Chevalier.

An' Charlie, he's my darling,
My darling, my darling,
Charlie, he's my darling,
The young Chevalier! –

Wi' Hieland bonnets on their heads,
And claymores bright and clear,
They came to fight for Scotland's right,
And the young Chevalier.

As he was walking up the street,
The city for to view,
O there he spied a bonnie lass
The window looking thro'.

They've left their bonnie Hieland hills,
Their wives and bairnies dear,
To draw the sword for Scotland's lord,
The young Chevalier.

Sae light's he jimped up the stair,
An' tirled at the pin;   *rattled*
And wha sae ready as hersel
To let the laddie in.

Oh, there were mony beating hearts,
And mony a hope and fear,
And mony were the prayers put up
For the young Chevalier.

He set his Jenny on his knee,
All in his Highland dress;
For brawlie weel he ken'd the way
To please a bonnie lass.

Oh, Charlie is my darling,
My darling, my darling;
Charlie is my darling,
The young Chevalier.

It's up yon heathery mountain,
And down yon scroggy glen,   *covered with stunted bushes*
We daur na gang a milking,
For Charlie and his men.

Moderate

Bon - nie Char - lie's noo a - wa', Safe - ly ower the friend - ly main;

Mo - ny a heart will break in twa Should he ne'er come back a - gain.

Will ye no come back a - gain? Will ye no come back a - gain?

Bet - ter lo'ed ye can - na be;— Will ye no come back a - gain?

con Ped.

CHORUS AFTER EACH VERSE

Bonnie Charlie's noo awa',
Safely ower the friendly main;
Mony a heart will break in twa
Should he ne'er come back again.

Will ye no come back again?
Will ye no come back again?
Better lo'ed ye canna be; –
Will ye no come back again?

Ye trusted in your Hieland men; –
They trusted you, dear Charlie;
They kent you hiding in the glen,
Death and exile braving.

English bribes were a' in vain.
Though puir and puirer we maun be,
Siller canna buy the hearts
That beat aye for thine and thee.

We watched thee in the gloamin' hour,   *twilight*
We watched thee in the morning grey;
Though thirty thousand pounds they'd gi'e,
Oh, there is nane that would betray!

Sweet the laverock's note and lang,   *lark's*
Lilting wildly up the glen;
But aye to me he sings ae sang –
Will ye no come back again?

Will ye no come back again?
Will ye no come back again?
Better lo'ed ye canna be; –
Will ye no come back again?

Lady Nairne (born Carolina Oliphant in 1766) came from a staunchly Jacobite background on both sides – her father, Laurence Oliphant, was an aide-de-camp of the Young Pretender in the '45 who carried the news of the Battle of Prestonpans to Edinburgh. Carolina's family had all suffered in the Stewart cause, but that of her husband, Captain Nairne, even more so, for they endured exile, forfeiture of wealth and rank, and the destruction of their family home. Captain Nairne was obliged as a result to live off his pay as an army officer in Ireland and the two were not able to marry until she was forty-one and he fifty. Even so, they managed to produce one child who remained bitter about the 'reverses of his House' and his lost inheritance. Sadly he died young, of influenza, while travelling on the Continent with his mother in pursuit of good health. Lady Nairne's Jacobite songs are more truly felt than those of James Hogg, whose nostalgia for the '45 was mostly a romantic pose. 'Will ye no come back again?' is an adaptation of an older Jacobite song, a perennial favourite which is sung affectionately (and often tearfully) by exiled Scots all over the world.

SPEED BONNIE BOAT *SIR HAROLD BOULTON*

REPEAT CHORUS AFTER EACH VERSE

Speed bonnie boat like a bird on the wing,
Onward the sailors cry;
Carry the lad that's born to be king
Over the sea to Skye.

Loud the winds howl, loud the waves roar,
Thunderclaps rend the air;
Baffled our foes stand by the shore,
Follow they will not dare.

Though the waves leap, soft shall ye sleep,
Ocean's a royal bed.
Rocked in the deep Flora will keep
Watch by your weary head.

Many's the lad fought on that day
Well the claymore could wield,
When the night came silently lay
Dead on Culloden's field.

Burned are our homes, exile and death
Scatter the loyal men;
Yet ere the sword cool in the sheath
Charlie will come again.

Speed bonnie boat like a bird on the wing,
Onward the sailors cry;
Carry the lad that's born to be king
Over the sea to Skye.

Annie MacLeod (later Lady Wilson) heard the first part of this tune in 1879 while being rowed from Torrin to Loch Coruisk, in Skye. She added the second part herself and in 1884 Sir Harold Boulton (editor of Songs of the North*) wrote the words which have so caught the popular imagination. They refer to an episode during the wanderings of Prince Charles in the winter of 1745–6, when he escaped from his enemies by putting out to sea with Flora Macdonald and a few loyal Highlanders. A storm was rising and his pursuers chose not to follow although they were well-equipped with boats.*

Stevenson's evocative song of lost youth dates from 1887. The writing of "Over the sea to Skye", wrote his wife, 'grew out of a visit from one of the last of the old school of Scots Gentlewomen, Miss Ferrier, a granddaughter of Professor Wilson (Christopher North). Her singing was a great delight to my husband, who would beg for song after song, especially the Jacobite airs, which had to be repeated several times. The words to one of these seemed unworthy, so he made a new set of verses more in harmony with the plaintive tune.' As a youth Stevenson had enjoyed boating holidays on Skye and the Western Isles where his engineer father built lighthouses. Forced by bad health to leave Scotland for Samoa, the novelist regretted he had not been a man of action and sympathized with the elderly Charles Stewart dying in Rome, a drunken sot hardly able to believe he had once been young, adventurous, hopeful and admired. 'Over the sea to Skye' was found written out with the music in Stevenson's library after his death.

Sing me a song of a lad that is gone,
Say, could that lad be I?
Merry of soul he sailed on a day
Over the sea to Skye.

Mull was astern, Rum on the port,
Eigg on the starboard bow;
Glory of youth glowed in his soul:
Where is that glory now?

Give me again all that was there,
Give me the sun that shone!
Give me the eyes, give me the soul,
Give me the lad that's gone!

Billow and breeze, islands and seas,
Mountains of rain and sun,
All that was good, all that was fair,
All that was me is gone.

Sing me a song of a lad that is gone,
Say, could that lad be I?
Merry of soul he sailed on a day
Over the sea to Skye.

O, I am come to the low countrie –		I was the happiest of a' the Clan,	
Ochon, Ochon, Ochrie! –	*alas*	Sair, sair may I repine;	*sore*
Without a penny in my purse		For Donald was the brawest man,	*handsomest*
To buy a meal to me.		And Donald he was mine.	

O, I am come to the low countrie –
Ochon, Ochon, Ochrie! –   *alas*
Without a penny in my purse
To buy a meal to me.

It was na sae in the Highland hills,
Ochon, Ochon, Ochrie!
Nae woman in the Country wide
Sae happy was as me.

For then I had a score o' kye,   *of cattle*
Ochon, Ochon, Ochrie!
Feeding on yon hill sae high,
And giving milk to me.

And there I had three score o' yowes,   *of ewes*
Ochon, Ochon, Ochrie!
Skipping on yon bonnie knowes,   *fair hillocks*
And casting wo to me.   *wool*

I was the happiest of a' the Clan,
Sair, sair may I repine;   *sore*
For Donald was the brawest man,   *handsomest*
And Donald he was mine.

Till Charlie Stewart came at last,
Sae far to set us free;
My Donald's arm was wanted then
For Scotland and for me.

Their waefu' fate what need I tell,   *woeful*
Right to the wrang did yield;
My Donald and his Country fell
Upon Culloden field.

Ochon, O, Donald, O!
Ochon, Ochon, Ochrie!
Nae woman in the warld wide
Sae wretched now as me.

Burns wrote these verses to an old Gaelic air, 'The Highland widow's lament', which he learned from a lady in the north of Scotland. They appeared in the Scots Musical Museum *(vol. I, no. 89) in 1796. Only the refrain 'Ochon, Ochon, Ochrie!' is traditional. Robert Schumann was impressed by the tune, using it in his* Liederkreis, Opus 25.

LASSIES
WANT
LADS

REPEAT CHORUS AFTER EACH VERSE

Tha mi sgìth 's mì leam fhìn,
Buain na rainich, buain na rainich,
Tha mi sgìth 's mi leam fhìn
Buain na rainich daonnan.

Cùl an tomain, bràigh an tomain,
Cùl an tomain bhòidhich,
Cùl an tomain, bràigh an tomain,
H-uile latha 'm ònar.

'S tric a bha mi fhìn 's mo leannan
Anns a' ghleannan cheòthar
'G èisdeachd còisir bhinn an doire
Seinn 'sa' choille dhòmhail.

'S bochd nach robh mi leat a rithist,
Sinn a bhiodh ceòlmhor;
Rachainn leat gu cùl na cruinne,
Air bhàrr tuinne seòladh.

Ciod am feum dhomh bhith ri tuireadh;
Dè ni tuireadh dhòmh-sa,
'S mi cho fada o gach duine
B'urrainn tigh'nn g'am chòmhnadh?

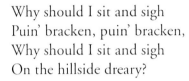

There are several versions of this plaintive Hebridean pentatonic song. The Gaelic says: I am tired of being alone,/ pulling bracken, pulling bracken./ Often my lover and I were in a misty valley/ listening to the melodious choir of the thicket/ playing in a dense wood.// Sad that I am not with you,/ 'Tis we who would be tuneful.// James Hogg (1770–1835) uses poetic license in the version below, making it a 'Fairy's love song' published in Albyn's Anthology *(1816) and Marjory Kennedy-Fraser's* Songs of the Hebrides *(1909). The tune, entitled 'Eilidh Bhan', occurs in 19th-century collections with Gaelic words by Evan MacColl, the Lochfyne bard born in 1808, and a translation by Malcolm MacFarlane: Alie Bain o' the glen,/ Bonnie lassie, bonnie lassie;/ Alie Bain o' the glen,/ Wha could help but lo'e her?*

Why should I sit and sigh
Puin' bracken, puin' bracken,
Why should I sit and sigh
On the hillside dreary?

When I see the plover rising
Or the curlew wheeling,
Then I trow my mortal lover
Back to me is stealing.

Why should I sit and sigh
Puin' bracken, puin' bracken,
Why should I sit and sigh
All alone and weary?

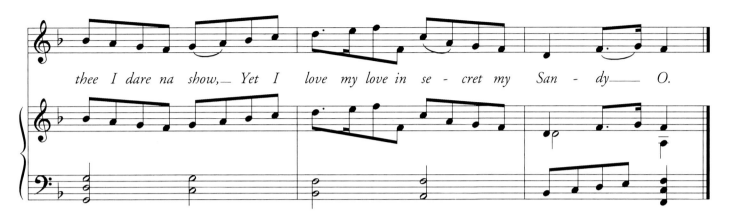

thee I dare na show,— Yet I love my love in se - cret my San - dy— O.

My Sandy gi'ed to me a ring,
Was a' beset wi' diamonds fine;
But I gi'ed him a far better thing,
I gi'ed my heart in pledge o' his ring.

My Sandy O, my Sandy O,
My bonny, bonny Sandy O;
Tho' the love that I owe to thee I dare na show,
Yet I love my love in secret my Sandy O.

My Sandy brak a piece o' gowd,
While down his cheeks the saut tears row'd;
He took a hauf and gi'ed it to me,
And I'll keep it till the hour I die.

My Sandy O, my Sandy O,
My bonny, bonny Sandy O;
Tho' the love that I owe to thee I dare na show,
Yet I love my love in secret my Sandy O.

The air appeared in Playford's Scotch Tunes *in 1700, and in both McGibbon's and Oswald's* Scots Tunes *(1742). The version above is from Johnson's* Scots Musical Museum *of 1790 (vol. III, no. 204) which gives alternative words which elevate the lovers socially while changing the sex of the singer:*

The smiling plains profusely gay,
 Are dress'd in all the pride of May,
The birds on ev'ry spray above,
To rapture wake the vocal grove.

But ah Miranda without thee,
Nor spring nor summer smiles on me,
 All lonely in the secret shade;
I mourn thy absence, charming maid.'

Like many Scots songs this was used instrumentally. It is one of an intriguing potpourri of both classical and folk tunes contained in James Thomson's 1702 manuscript-book of pieces for solo recorder (National Library of Scotland).

ROBIN ADAIR

Expressive

con Ped.

What's this dull town to me? Ro - bin's— not— near;

What was't I wish'd to see, What— wish'd— to— hear?

Where all the joy and mirth Made this— town— heav'n on earth?

Oh, they're— all— fled— wi' thee, Ro - bin— A - dair.

What's this dull town to me?
Robin's not near;
What was't I wish'd to see,
What wish'd to hear?
Where all the joy and mirth
Made this town heav'n on earth?
Oh, they're all fled wi' thee,
Robin Adair.

What made th'assembly shine?
Robin Adair;
What made the ball so fine?
Robin Adair.
What when the play was o'er,
What made my heart so sore?
O, it was parting with
Robin Adair.

But now thou'rt cold to me,
Robin Adair;
But now thou'rt cold to me,
Robin Adair.
Yet he I lov'd so well,
Still in my heart shall dwell;
Oh, I can ne'er forget
Robin Adair.

'It belongs [Robin Adair] to a class of gems which bear the impress of remote antiquity' wrote Colin Brown in The Thistle *at the end of the last century. 'Few of such peerless beauty can be found in music, so simple of construction, and so full of power and pathos.' Burns however found it troublesome to set: 'I likewise tried my hand on Robin Adair, and you will probably think with little success;' he wrote to his publisher George Thomson, 'but it is such a damned cramp, out-of-the-way measure, that I despair of doing anything better to it.' That one was 'Phyllis the fair' but he made another attempt ('Had I a cave on some wild distant shore') a year later, which pleased him better. The Gaelic name is Ceud mìle fàilte, Eilean mo rùin (A hundred thousand welcomes, island of my love) and the song is included in various 18th-century collections. There are several variants. An Irish version was anglicized as Eileen Aroon – 'Eileen of my love'.*

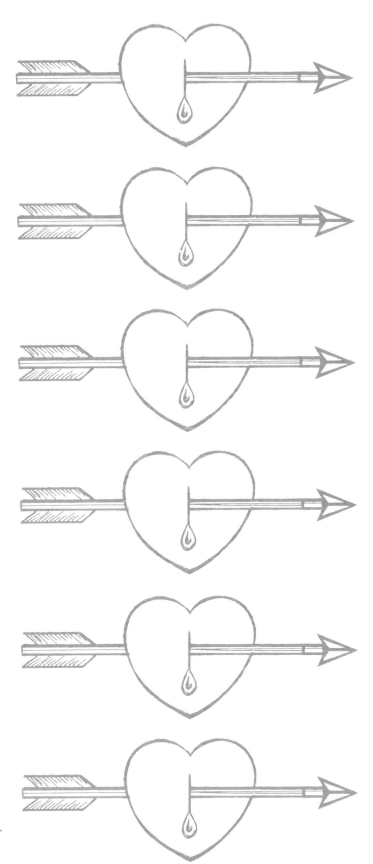

Moderate

con Ped.

My— heart is a-break-ing, dear Tit-tie, Some coun-sel un-to me come len': To—

an-ger them a' is a pi-ty, But what will I do wi' Tam Glen? I'm

think-ing, wi' sic a braw fel-low, In poor-tith I might mak a fen': What—

care I in rich-es to wal-low, If I mau-na mar-ry Tam Glen?

My heart is a-breaking, dear Tittie,   *sister*
Some counsel unto me come len':
To anger them a' is a pity,
But what will I do wi' Tam Glen?

I'm thinking, wi' sic a braw fellow,
In poortith I might mak a fen':   *poverty/ make do*
What care I in riches to wallow,
If I mauna marry Tam Glen?

There's Lowrie the laird o' Dumeller,
'Gude day to you brute' he comes ben:
He brags and he blaws o' his siller,   *boasts*
But when will he dance like Tam Glen?

My Minnie does constantly deave me,   *mother deafens*
And bids me beware o' young men;
They flatter, she says, to deceive me,
But wha can think sae o' Tam Glen?

My daddie says, gin I'll forsake him,
He'll gie me gude hunder marks ten:
But, if it's ordain'd I maun take him,
O wha will I get but Tam Glen?

Yestreen at the Valentines' dealing,
My heart to my mou gied a sten;   *leap*
For thrice I drew ane without failing,
And thrice it was written, Tam Glen.

The last Halloween I was waukin
My droukit sark-sleeve, as ye ken;   *drenched shirt*
His likeness cam up the house staukin,
And the very grey breeks o' Tam Glen.

Come counsel, dear Tittie, don't tarry:
I'll gie you my bonnie black hen,
Gif ye will advise me to marry
The lad I lo'e dearly, Tam Glen.

Of this song (Scots Musical Museum vol. III, no. 296) Burns wrote to Mrs Dunlop in 1788: 'I shall give you a song I finished the other day . . . It sings to an excellent old lilt, known in Oswald's Collection of Scots Music by the name of, "The merry beggars" – I would give a bottle of wine to hear it sung . . .' The song however was 'very early divorced from its proper tune'

in favour of 'The muckin o' Geordie's byre' , one of Burns's favourites. 'Valentines' dealing' was the traditional St Valentine's game by which young people discovered their future sweethearts. Burns explained 'droukit sark-sleeve': 'you go out, one or more (for this is a social spell) to a south-running spring or rivulet, where three lairds' lands meet, and dip your shirt sleeve. Go to bed in sight of a fire, and hang your wet sleeve before it to dry. Lie awake; and some time near midnight, an apparition, having the exact figure of the grand object in question, will come and turn the sleeve, as if to dry it.'

My Daddy's a Delver of Dykes,
My Minny can card and spin,   *mother*
And I'm a bonny young Lass,
And the Siller comes linkin in.   *briskly*
The Siller comes linkin in,
And it is fou fair to see,
And it's wow, wow, wow,   *Oh!*
What ails the Lads at me?

When ever our Bauty does bark,   *dog*
Then fast to the Door I do rin,
To see gin ony young Spark
Will light and venture in:
But ne'er a ane comes in,
Tho' mony a ane goes by,
Syne ben the House I rin,
And a weary Wight am I.   *person*

I had an auld Wife to my Minny,
And (wow) gin she keept me lang;
But now the Carlin's dead,   *old woman*
And I'll do what I can,
And I'll do what I can;
Wi' my twenty Pound and my Cow;
But wow it's an unco' thing,   *odd*
That na body comes to woe.

In Thomson's Orpheus Caledonius *of 1733 (vol. I, no. 33) the song given with this tune is 'My Daddy's a delver of Dykes' but Herd has the following fragment in his* Scots Songs *(1769): The mucking of Geordie's byre,/ And shooling the grupe [shovelling out the gutter] sae clean,/ Has gar'd me weit my cheeks/ And greit with baith my een [made her cry].// Chorus: It was ne'er my father's will,/ Nor yet my mother's desire,/ That e'er I should file my fingers/ Wi' mucking of Geordie's byre.// The mouse is a merry beast,/ And the moudiewart [mole] wants the een:/ But the warld shall ne'er get witt/ Sae merry as we hae been.//*

Moderate

How blyth was I each morn to see My swain come o'er the hill! He leap'd the burn, and flew to me: I met him wi' good will. *O the broom, the bon-ny bon-ny Broom, The Broom of the Cow - den - knows! I wish I were wi'*

my___ dear___ swain, Wi' his pipe____ and___ my___ ewes.

CHORUS AFTER EACH VERSE

How blyth was I each morn to see
My swain come o'er the hill!
He leap'd the burn, and flew to me:
I met him wi' good will.

O the broom, the bonny Broom,
The Broom of the Cowdenknows!
I wish I were wi' my dear swain,
Wi' his pipe and my ewes.

I neither wanted ewe nor lamb
While his flock near me lay;
He gather'd in my sheep at night,
And chear'd me a' the day.

He tun'd his pipe and reed sae sweet,
The birds stood list'ning by;
Ev'n the dull cattle stood and gaz'd,
Charm'd wi' his melody.

While thus we spent our time, by turns,
Betwixt our flocks and play:
I envy'd not the fairest dame,
Tho' ne'er so rich and gay.

Hard fate! that I shou'd banish'd be,
Gang heavily and mourn,
Because I lov'd the kindest swain,
That ever yet was born!

He did oblige me ev'ry hour;
Cou'd I but faithfu' be?
He staw my Heart: cou'd I refuse
Whate'er he ask'd of me?

My doggie, and my little kit,   *wooden bowl*
That held my wee soup whey,
My plaidy, broach and crooked stick,
May now ly useless by.

Adieu, ye Cowdenknows, adieu;
Farewell a' pleasures there;
Ye Gods, restore to me my swain,
Is a' I crave or care.

The estate of Cowdenknowes is on the east bank of the Leader Water near Melrose. The Knowes, or low hills, were renowned for their luxuriant growth of broom (a plant with erotic associations in Scottish folksong), which was apparently so tall that a man on horseback could ride through without being seen. This ballad comes from the Scots Musical Museum of 1787 (vol. I, no. 69) but it appears earlier, in William Thomson's Orpheus Caledonius of 1733 (vol. I, no.10), with the chorus: 'O the Broom, the bonny Broom,/ The Broom of Cowdenknows;/ I wish I were at hame again, To milk my Daddy's Ews.'// Scott's Minstrelsy of the Scottish Border (1802–03) tells of the shepherdess's seduction by a passing horseman. The story ends with the gentleman riding by next year and spotting the girl with her baby: 'Than he's leapd off his berry-brown steed,/ An he's set that fair may on:/ Caw out your kye, gude father, yoursel,/ For she's never caw them out again. // I am the laird of the Oakland hills/ I hae thirty plows and three/ An I hae gotten the bonniest lass/ That's in a' the south country.'//

Moderate

con Ped.

[There's] three score o' No-bles rade up the King's ha', But_ bon-nie Glen-o-gie's the_ flow'r o' them a'; Wi' his milk-white_ steed, and his bon-nie black_ e'e, 'Glen-o-gie, dear Mi-ther, Glen-o-gie for me!'

Three score o' Nobles rade up the King's ha',
But bonnie Glenogie's the flow'r o' them a';
Wi' his milk-white steed, and his bonnie black e'e,
'Glenogie, dear Mither, Glenogie for me!'

O Had your tongue, dochter,
                    ye'll get better than he,
O say na sae, mither, for that canna be;
Tho' Drumlie is richer and greater than he,
Yet if I maun tak him, I'll certainly dee.

Where will I get a bonnie boy, to win hose and shoon,
Will gae to Glenogie, and cum shune again?
O here am I, a bonnie boy, to win hose and shoon,
Will gae to Glenogie, and cum shune again.

When he gaed to Glenogie, 'twas wash and go dine;
'Twas wash ye, my pretty boy, wash and go dine;
O 'twas ne'er my Faither's fashion,
                    and it ne'er shall be mine,
To gar a Lady's hasty errand wait till I dine.

But there is, Glenogie, a letter to thee;
The first line that he read, a low smile gae he;
The next line that he read, the tear blindit his e'e;
But the last line that he read, he gart the table flee.

Gar saddle the black horse, gae saddle the brown;
Gar saddle the swiftest steed e'er rade frae a town;
But lang ere the horse was drawn,
                    and brought to the green,
O bonnie Glenogie was twa mile his lane.

When he cam to Glenfeldy's door, little mirth was there,
Bonnie Jeannie's Mother was tearing her hair;
Ye're welcome, Glenogie, ye're welcome! said she;
Ye're welcome, Glenogie, your Jeannie to see.

Pale and wan was she, when Glenogie gaed ben;
But red and rosy grew she whene'er he sat down;
She turned awa her head,
                    but the smile was in her e'e;
O binna feared Mother, I'll may be no dee.

This is the first printed version of the ballad of 'Glenlogie, or Jean of Bethelnie' – from Smith's The Scottish Minstrel *(1822–24). Here the hero is Glenogie (without the 'l'). Traditionally, Jeannie was one Jane, daughter of the Laird of Bethelnie, who happened to catch sight of Sir George Gordon of Glenlogie as he rode through Banchory one day. The girl fell desperately in love with him and sent him a letter stating her case, but when it came to her ears that he was making fun of her she became seriously ill. Her father's chaplain, who was 'no doubt bred in the court of Cupid', undertook the correspondence, and was more successful. Jane, then only in her fifteenth year, was married shortly afterwards to the object of her desires.*

CHORUS AFTER EACH VERSE

My Mither's ay glow'rin owre me,   scowling
Though she did the same before me;
I canna get leave
To look at my love,
Or else she'd be like to devour me.

Right fain wad I tak' your offer,
Sweet sir, but I'll tine my tocher; *lose my dowry*
Then, Sandy, you'll fret,
And wyte your poor Kate,   *blame*
Whene'er you keek in your toom coffer. *look/empty*

For though my father has plenty
O' siller and plenishing dainty,
Yet he's unco swear   *reluctant*
To twine wi' his gear;   *part with his money*
And sae we had need to be tenty. *careful*

Tutor my parents wi' caution,
Be wylie in ilka motion;
Brag weel o' your land,
And there's a leal hand,   *faithful*
Win them, I'll be at your devotion.

Allan Ramsay published these verses entitled 'Katy's answer' in 1724 in the Tea-Table Miscellany, *a four-volume collection (1723–c.1737) of specially manufactured, or suitably modified, Scots songs intended for use in the fashionable drawing-rooms of Edinburgh and London. Ramsay was no musician and the* Miscellany *was published without music – he expected the songs to be sung unaccompanied to existing folk tunes – so his chagrin was great when two years after the first volume came out William Thomson published* Orpheus Caledonius, *a collection of fifty Scots songs set for voice with bass line, thirty-eight of them lifted straight from the* Miscellany. *The fact that the musical settings were extremely tasteful, reflecting Thomson's sensitivity as a singer, was of little consolation to the poet, but he got his own back on the publisher by plundering from the remaining dozen songs of* Orpheus Caledonius *for* Tea-Table Miscellany, *vol. II, which came out shortly afterwards. This tune, 'A health to Betty', appears in Playford's* Dancing Master, *1651.*

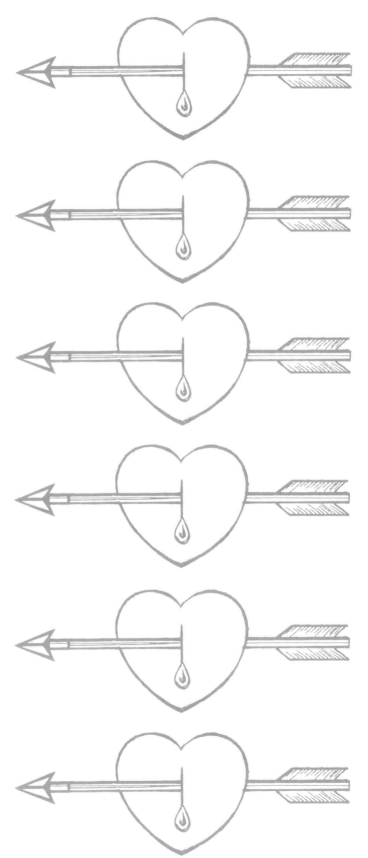

Moderate

Why weep ye by the tide, la-dye? Why weep ye by the tide?___ I'll

con Ped.

wed ye to my youn-gest son, And ye shall be his bride. And

ye shall be his bride, la-dye, Sae come-ly to___ be seen— But

aye she loot the tears down fa', for Jock o' Ha-zel-dean.

Why weep ye by the tide, ladye?
Why weep ye by the tide?
I'll wed ye to my youngest son,
And ye shall be his bride.
And ye shall be his bride, ladye,
Sae comely to be seen –
But aye she loot the tears down fa',
For Jock o' Hazeldean.

Now let this wilfu' grief be done,
And dry that cheek so pale,
Young Frank is chief of Errington,
And lord of langley-dale.
His step is first in peaceful ha',
His sword in battle keen –
But aye she loot the tears down fa',
For Jock o' Hazeldean.

A chain o' gold ye shall not lack,
Nor braid to bind your hair,
Nor mettled hound, nor managed hawk,
Nor palfrey fresh and fair;
And you, the foremost o' them a',
Shall ride our forest queen –
But aye she loot the tears down fa',
For Jock o' Hazeldean.

The kirk was deck'd at morning tide,
The taper glimmer'd fair,
The priest and bridegroom wait the bride,
And dame and knight are there.
They sought her baith by bower and ha',
The ladye was not seen;
She's ower the border, and awa
Wi' Jock o' Hazeldean.

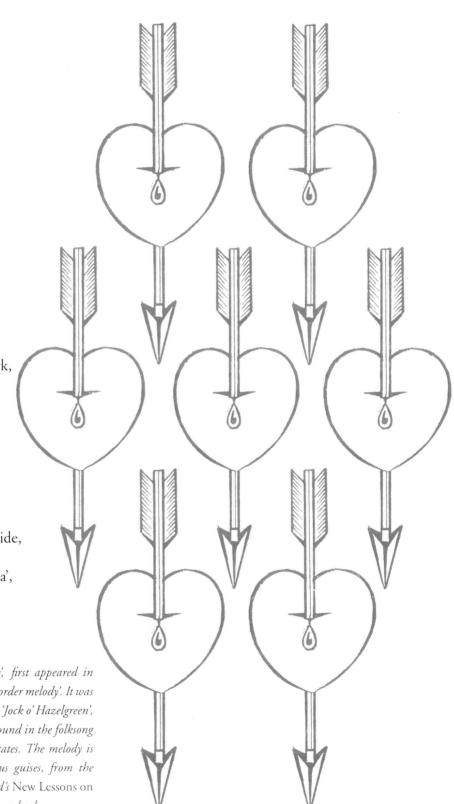

This ballad, which some consider 'too literary', first appeared in Campbell's Albyn's Anthology *(1816) set to 'a Border melody'. It was based on an earlier ballad, 'Jock o'Hazeldean', or 'Jock o' Hazelgreen', of which there are many variants, several to be found in the folksong tradition of the southern states of the United States. The melody is older than the ballad and crops up in various guises, from the midseventeenth century onwards, e.g. in Playford's* New Lessons on the Gittern, *1652, and in many of the later song-books.*

SKULDUGGERY AND SUDDEN DEATH

Slow and expressive

Ye Hie-lands and ye Law-lands,— O, whar ha'e ye been? They ha'e

slain the Earl o' Mur-ray And laid him on the green. He was a braw

gal-lant, And he rade— at the ring; And the bon-nie Earl o' Mur-ray, He

micht ha'e been a King. O, lang will his la - dy look frae the Cas - tle

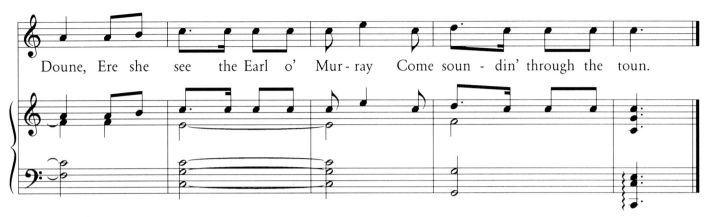

Doune, Ere she see the Earl o' Mur-ray Come soun-din' through the toun.

Ye Hielands and ye Lawlands,	O, wae betide ye, Huntly,
O, whar ha'e ye been?	And wherefore did ye sae?
They ha'e slain the Earl o' Murray,	I bade ye bring him wi' you,
And laid him on the green.	And forebad' ye him to slay.
He was a braw gallant, *handsome*	He was a braw gallant,
And he rade at the ring; *rode*	And he played at the glove;
And the bonnie Earl o' Murray	And the bonnie Earl o' Murray,
He micht ha'e been a king.	He was the Queen's love.
O, lang will his lady look frae the Castle Doune	O, lang will his lady look frae the Castle Doune
Ere she see the Earl o' Murray	Ere she see the Earl o' Murray
Come soundin' through the toun.	Come soundin' through the toun.

Doune Castle was the Murray family stronghold. 'The seventh of Febry, this zeire, 1592', writes Balfour (Annals of Scotland), 'the Earle of Murray was cruelly murthered by the Earle of Huntley, at his house in Dunibrissel, in Fyffe-shyre . . . It was given out and publickly tackt, that the Earle of Huntley was only the instrument of perpetrating this facte, to satisfie the King's jealosie of Murray, quhome the Queene more rashely than wisely, some few days before, had commendit in the king's hearing with too many epithets of a proper and gallant man.' There is no historical evidence of an amorous connection between James Stewart, the Earl, and the Queen, Anne of Denmark, though the Earl was 'a comely personage of great stature' well deserving of the title 'Bonnie'. The likely pretext for the murder was Murray's connection with the Earl of Bothwell, who had tried to kidnap King James two months earlier. The tune given is a modern one, published in the 1920s. The following was first printed in 1733 by William Thomson, a professional singer and publisher known in Court circles for 'the sweetness of his voice, and the agreeable manner in which he sung a Scots song'. Its vocal range of an octave and a sixth is wide even by Scots song standards – possibly why it has fallen out of favour. The trills and grace notes embellishing it are no doubt characteristic of Thomson's own performing style.

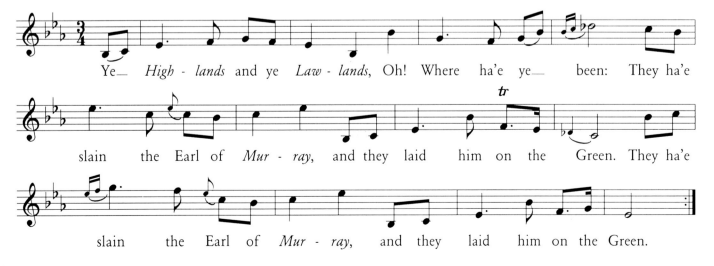

Ye— High-lands and ye Law-lands, Oh! Where ha'e ye— been: They ha'e slain the Earl of Mur-ray, and they laid him on the Green. They ha'e slain the Earl of Mur-ray, and they laid him on the Green.

THE TWA CORBIES

Lively

As I was walk - ing all a - lane,— I heard twa cor - bies mak - ing mane.— The tane un - to the t'i - ther say,— Whare sall we gang and dine the day? *Fald, the lal, the lal, the ley;— Fald, the lal, the lal, the ley.—*

con Ped.

CHORUS AFTER EACH VERSE

As I was walking all alane,
I heard twa corbies making mane.   *two ravens talk drearily*
The tane unto the t'ither say,
Whare sall we gang and dine the day?

Fald, the lal, the lal, the ley:
Fald, the lal, the lal, the ley.

In behint yon auld fail dyke   *old turf wall*
I wot there lies a new slain knight;
Naebody kens that he lies there
But his hawk, his hound, and his lady fair.

His hound is to the hunting gane
His hawk to fetch the wild-fowl hame,
His lady's ta'en anither mate,
So we may mak' our dinner sweet.

Ye'll sit on his white hause-bane,   *collar bone*
And I'll pyke oot his bonny blue e'en;   *pick*
Wi' ae lock o' his gowden hair
We'll theek oor nest when it grows bare,   *thatch*

There's mony a ane for him maks mane
But nane shall ken whare he is gane,
O'er his white banes, when they are bare
The wind sall blaw for evermair.

Expressive

There are several versions (words and music) of this stark, grisly ballad, the earliest text of which is printed, with the music, in Ravenscroft's Melismata *of 1611. This one was given to Sir Walter Scott for his* Minstrelsy of the Scottish Border *(1802–3) by his friend Charles Kirkpatrick Sharpe, who took it down from a lady's recitation, and the tune comes (with an added refrain) from George Eyre-Todd's* Ancient Scots Ballads *of 1894. Various traditional tunes in both major and minor keys have been used as settings for what the scholar and ballad collector, Professor Child, called 'a cynical variation on the theme of devoted love' though in recent years 'The Twa Corbies' has often been sung to the lovely old Breton melody, 'An Alarc'h' (The Swan), which is highly effective in its simplicity. Incidentally, in English forms of the ballad (e.g. 'The Three Ravens'), the knight's hawk, hound and lady display greater devotion.*

The gypsies came to our Lord's yett,   *gate*
And vow but they sang sweetly;
They sang sae sweet, and sae compleat,
That down came the fair lady.
When she came tripping down the stair,
And a' her maids before her;
As soon as they saw her weel fair'd face,
They coost the glamer o'er her.   *cast a spell*

Gae tak frae me this gay mantile,
And bring to me a plaidie;
For if kith and kin and a' had sworn,
I'll follow the gypsie laddie.
Yestreen I lay in a weel-made bed,
And my good lord beside me;
This night I'll ly in a tenant's barn,
Whatever shall betide me.

Oh! come to your bed says Johny Faa,
Oh! come to your bed, my deary;
For I vow and swear by the hilt of my sword,
That your lord shall nae mair come near ye.
I'll go to bed to my Johny Faa,
And I'll go to bed to my deary;
For I vow and swear by what past yestreen,
That my lord shall nae mair come near me.

I'll make a hap to my Johny Faa,   *cover*
And I'll make a hap to my deary;
And he's get a' the coat gaes round,
And my lord shall nae mair come near me.
And when our lord came hame at e'en,
And speir'd for his fair lady,   *asked*
The tane she cry'd, and the other reply'd,   *one*
She's awa wi' the gypsie laddie.

Gae saddle to me the black, black steed,
Gae saddle and mak him ready;
Before that I either eat or sleep,
I'll gae seek my fair lady.
And we were fifteen well made men,
Altho' we were nae bonny;
And we are a' put down for ane,   *hanged for one*
The earl of Cassilis' lady.

'Johny Faa, or *The Gypsie Laddie'* is in Johnson's Scots Musical Museum *of 1788 (vol. II, no. 181) with this note attached to the index: 'Neighbouring tradition strongly vouches for the truth of this story.' Robert Burns wrote that 'the castle is still remaining at Maybole where his lordship shut up his wayward spouse and kept her for life' and traditionally the location of the incident in the ballad was Cassilis House, on the banks of the Doon. This 14th-century tower is now the home of the Marquis of Ailsa and although the building was altered in the 17th and 19th centuries, a prison cell built into the 16ft (5m) thick north wall is one of the original features. The story goes that the wanton Countess of Cassilis was brought back from her flight with her lover, Sir John Fall, who was disguised as a gypsy, and forced to witness the hanging of the entire gypsy party, her lover included, on the Dule-tree (tree of sorrow) which stood in front of the house. A version of the melody appears in the Skene MS, 1615–20, under the title 'Ladie Cassilles Lilt' and this one is well-known set to William Glen's verses 'Wae's me for Prince Charlie'.*

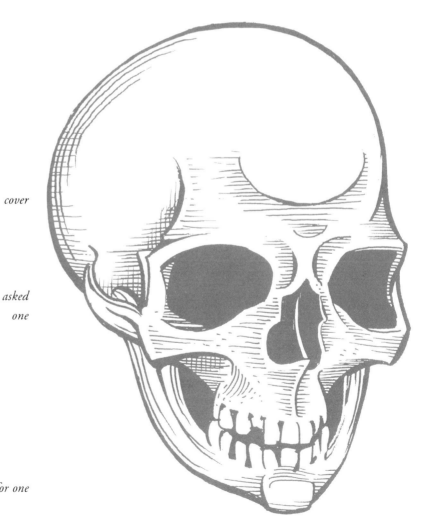

Moderate

It fell on a day, a bon - ny sim - mer day, When the corn grew_ green_ and

yel - low, That_ there fell_ out a great dis - pute Be -

tween Ar - gyle_ and_ Air - lie, That there_ fell_ out a

great dis - pute Be - tween Ar - gyle_ and_ Air - lie.

REPEAT LAST TWO LINES AFTER EACH VERSE

It fell on a day, a bonny simmer day,
When the leaves were green and yellow,
That there fell out a great dispute
Between Argyle and Airlie.

Argyle he has taen a hundred o' his men,
A hundred men and fifty,
And he's awa, on yon green shaw,   *small wood, thicket*
To plunder the bonny house o' Airlie.

The lady looked owre the hie castle wa';
And oh! but she sighed sairly,
When she saw Argyle and a' his men,
Come to plunder the bonny house o' Airlie.

'Come down to me,' said proud Argyle;
'Come down to me lady Airlie,
Or I swear by the sword I haud in my hand,
I winna leave a stanin stane in Airlie.'

'I'll no come down, ye proud Argyle,
Until that ye speak mair fairly,
Tho' ye swear by the sword that ye haud in your hand,
That ye winna leave a stanin stane in Airlie.'

'Had my ain lord been at his hame,
But he's awa wi' Charlie,
There's no a Campbell in a' Argyle,
Dare hae trod on the bonny green o' Airlie.'

'But since we can haud out nae mair,
My hand I offer fairly;
Oh! lead me down to yonder glen,
That I may nae see the burnin o' Airlie.'

He's taen her by the trembling hand,
But he's no taen her fairly,
For he led her up to a hie hill tap,
Where she saw the burnin o' Airlie.

Clouds o' smoke, and flames sae hie,
Soon left the wa's but barely;
And she laid her down on that hill to die,
When she saw the burnin o' Airlie.

This ballad commemorates an incident during the troubled reign of Charles the First (great-grandfather of the Bonnie Prince) and there are many variants. The Earl of Airlie remained staunchly royalist in opposition to the dominant Covenanting party, and was obliged to leave Scotland in 1640. While he was in England fighting for Charles, the Marquis of Argyle seized the opportunity to destroy the Earl's two principal seats, Airlie and Forther. There is no historical evidence pointing to sexual harassment of Airlie's daughter-in-law, Lady Margaret, by Argyle, but it was noted that the Marquis demonstrated a vindictive, personal hatred by attacking fine carved work and door lintels of Airlie with his own hands. Later however, he paid the debt of retributive justice for at the Restoration he was tried and condemned for political offences and beheaded on May 27, 1661. It was said though, that he died with great equanimity and fortitude. The tune is found in Gow's Sixth Collection *of 1782.*

The Duke o' Montrose has written to Argyle
To come in the morning early,
And lead his men to the back of Dunkeld,
To plunder the bonnie house o' Airlie.

The lady look'd o'er her window sae hie,
And oh! but she looked weary;
And there she spied the great Argyle,
Come to plunder the bonnie house o' Airlie.

'Come doun, come doun, Lady Margaret' he says,
'Come doun and kiss me fairly,
Or before the morning clear daylight
I'll no leave a standing stane in Airlie.'

'I wadna kiss thee, great Argyle,
I wadna kiss thee fairly;
I wadna kiss thee, great Argyle,
Gin ye shouldna leave a standing stane in Airlie.'

He has taen her by the middle sae sma',
Says, 'Lady where is your drury?'
'It's up and down the bonnie burn-side
Amang the planting o' Airlie.'

dowry

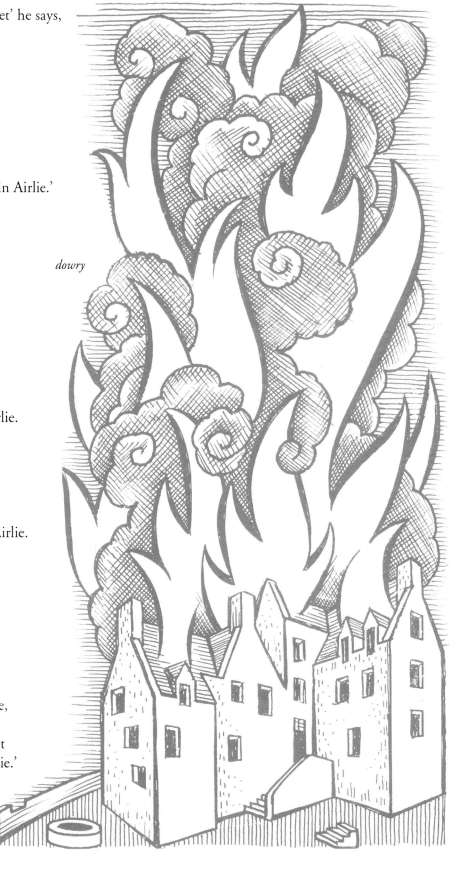

They sought it up, they sought it doun,
They sought it late and early,
And found it in the bonnie balm-tree
That shines on the bowling-green o' Airlie.

He has taen her by the left shoulder,
And oh! but she grat sairly;
And led her doun to yon green bank,
Till he plundered the bonnie house o' Airlie.

'O! it's I hae seven braw sons,' she says,
'And the youngest ne'er saw his daddie;
And although I had as mony mae,
I wad gie them a' to Charlie.

'But gin my gude lord had been at hame,
As this night he is wi' Charlie,
There durst na a Campbell in a' the west
Hae plundered the bonnie house o' Airlie.'

Hie upon Hielands, and laigh upon Tay,   *low*
Bonnie George Campbell rade out on a day;
He saddled, he bridled, and gallant rade he,
And hame cam' his guid horse, but never cam' he.

Out cam' his mother dear, greeting fu' sair;
And out cam' his bonnie bryde riving her hair; *tearing*
'My meadow lies green, the corn is unshorn,
My barn is to build, and my baby's unborn.'

This beautiful old ballad with its powerful rhythms may be a lament for an adherent of the house of Argyle who was killed at the battle of Glenlivet in 1594, though some believe it alludes to the murder of Campbell of Cawdor in 1591. In the second edition of The Scotish Minstrel *Smith (who first published the ballad with its tune in the 1820s) changed lines three and four of the second stanza to:* The meadow lies green, the corn is unshorn,/ But bonnie George Campbell will never return!// *and added a third verse:* Saddled and bridled and booted rade he,/ A plume in his helmet, a sword at his knee,/ But toom cam his saddle, all bloody to see,/ Oh, hame cam his guid horse but never cam he.//

Expressive

Wil - ly's rare___ and Wil - ly's fair, And Wil - ly's wond - 'rous___

bon - ny; And Wil - ly heght to___ mar - ry me, Gin___

e'er he marr - y'd on - y, oh! Gin e'er he marr - y'd on - y.

con Ped.

Willy's rare and Willy's fair,
And Willy's wond'rous bonny;
And Willy heght to marry me,   *promised*
Gin e'er he marry'd ony.

Yestreen I made my Bed fu' brade,
The night I'll make it narrow;
For a' the live-long Winter's Night
I lie twin'd of my Marrow.   *parted from my mate*

O came you by yon Water-side,
Pu'd you the Rose or Lilly;
Or came you by yon Meadow green,
Or saw you my sweet Willy?

She sought him East, she sought him West,
She sought him brade and narrow;   *far and near*
Sine in the cleaving of a Craig,
She found him drown'd in Yarrow.

She's ta'en three links of her yellow hair
That hung down long and yellow;
And she's tied it about sweet Willy's waist,
An' drawn him out of Yarrow.

This is the first printed version of the tune 'Willy's rare and Willy's Fair'. It appeared in Thomson's Orpheus Caledonius *of 1733 (vol. II, no. 49). The last verse is a later addition, from Cromek's* Scottish Songs *(1810). There are several variants of the famous old Border Ballad: 'Sweet Willy', 'Willie was drowned in Yarrow' and 'Nae birdies sang the mirky hour' to the tune 'Sweet Willy'. There is no historical evidence of a specific tragedy linked to the song, but Sir Walter Scott believed that it referred to John Scott, sixth son of the Laird of Harden, who was murdered by his kinsmen, the Scotts of Gilmancleugh, in Ettrick Forest. There is also a tradition that the hero was murdered by the brother either of his wife or his betrothed wife.*

O that I were where Helen lies!
Night and day on me she cries;
O that I were where Helen lies
In fair Kirkconnel lee.

O Helen fair beyond compare,
A ringlet of thy flowing hair,
I'll wear it still for ever mair
Untill the day I die.

Curs'd be the hand that shot the shot,
And curs'd the hand that gave the crack!
Into my arms bird Helen lap,   *dear*
And died for sake o' me.

O think na ye but my heart was sair;
My love fell down and spake nae mair;
There did she swoon wi' meikle care
On fair Kirkconnel lee.

I lighted down, my sword did draw,
I cutted him in pieces sma';
I cutted him in pieces sma'
On fair Kirkconnel lee.

O Helen chaste, thou'rt now at rest,
If I were with thee I were blest,
Where thou lies low and takes thy rest
On fair Kirkconnel lee.

I wish my grave was growing green,
A winding sheet put o'er my e'en,
And I in Helen's arms lying
In fair Kirkconnel lee!

I wish I were where Helen lies!
Night and day on me she cries:
O that I were where Helen lies
On fair Kirkconnel lee.

There are many versions of this traditional ballad which tells the romantic tale of Helen, Eelin or Ellen Irvine: this is the one which Burns contributed to the Scots Musical Museum *of 1788 (vol. II, no. 155). Thomas Pennant saw her grave or at least mentions it (he was not averse to lifting other writers' work) in his* Tour in Scotland *(1774) and gives the story: 'She was the daughter of the house of Kirkconnel; and was beloved by two gentlemen at the same time; the one vowed to sacrifice the successful rival to his resentment; and watched an opportunity while the happy pair were sitting on the banks of the Kirtle . . . Ellen . . . fondly thinking to save her favourite, interposed; and receiving the wound intended, fell and expired in his arms. He instantly revenged her death; then fled into Spain, and served for some time against the infidels: on his return he visited the grave . . . and expiring on the spot, was interred by her side . . . the tombstone, with his* hic jacet Adam Fleming *the only memorial of this unhappy gentleman, except an antient ballad of no great merit.' Burns was of the same opinion as to the ballad's merits, and wrote to publisher George Thomson in July 1793: 'The old ballad, "I wish I were where Helen lies", is silly to contemptibility. My alteration in Johnson is not much better. Mr Pinkerton, in what he calls* Ancient Ballads *has the best set. It is full of his own interpolations.' Scott also has a version and Wordsworth's (* Lyrical Ballads, *1896) reads like a parody: Fair Ellen Irwin, when she sate,/ Upon the braes of Kirtle,/ Was lovely as a Grecian Maid / A'dorn'd with wreaths of myrtle//.*

LORD RONALD

Fairly slow

O,— where hae ye— been,— Lord— Ron - ald, my— son? O,—

where hae— ye been,— Lord— Ron - ald,— my— son? I hae

been wi' my— sweet - heart, mo - ther, make my bed— soon, For I'm

wea - ry wi' the hunt - ing, and— fain wad lie— down.

con Ped.

O, where hae ye been, Lord Ronald, my son?
O, where hae ye been, Lord Ronald, my son?
I hae been wi' my sweetheart, mother, make my bed soon,
For I'm weary wi' the hunting, and fain wad lie down.

What got ye frae your sweetheart, Lord Ronald, my son?
What got ye frae your sweetheart, Lord Ronald, my son?
I hae got deadly poison, mother, make my bed soon;
For life is a burden that soon I'll lay down.

Burns contributed this fragment of a traditional ballad and its tune – the first of many variants – to the Scots Musical Museum *of 1792 (vol. 4, no. 327). Similar legends crop up in the folklore of Europe but Sir Walter Scott believed that the song referred to the death of Thomas Randolph, or Randal, Earl of Moray, who recaptured Edinburgh Castle from the English in 1314. After the death of Robert the Bruce he was made Guardian of the Kingdom during David II's minority, but while raising an army in 1332 to repel a threatened*

attack by the English, Randolph died suddenly and violently of suspected poisoning. 'This air,' wrote Burns, 'a very favourite one in Ayrshire, is evidently the original of "Lochaber". In this manner, most of our finest modern airs have had their origin. Some early minstrel, or musical shepherd, composed the simple, artless air, which being pickt up by the more learned modern musician took the improved form it bears.' It appears (as 'Lochaber no more') in Orpheus Caledonius *of 1733 (vol. II, no. 20).*

CHORUS AFTER EACH VERSE

Farewell, ye dungeons dark and strong,
The wretch's destinie!
McPherson's time will not be long,
On yonder gallows tree.

Sae rantingly, sae wantonly,   *so riotously*
Sae dauntingly gae'd he,   *went*
He play'd a spring, and danc'd it round   *lively tune*
Below the gallows tree.

O what is death but parting breath?
On many a bloody plain
I've dar'd his face, and in this place
I scorn him yet again!

Untie these bands from off my hands,
And bring to me my sword;
And there's no a man in all Scotland,
But I'll brave him at a word.

I've liv'd a life of sturt and strife;   *trouble*
I die by treacherie:
It burns my heart I must depart
And not avenged be.

Now farewell, light, thou sunshine bright,
And all beneath the sky!
May coward shame disdain his name,
The wretch that dares not die!

This is a traditional ballad reconstructed by Burns for the Scots Musical Museum *(vol. II, no. 114). James MacPherson, fiddler, was the son of a gentleman and a gypsy, who pursued a Robin Hood-type career in the late 17th century. He led a notorious gang of cattle-thieves in Morayshire and on 7 November 1700 he and three of his colleagues (two Browns, and a Gordon) were charged with being 'Egyptian rogues and vagabonds, of keeping the markets in their ordinary manner of thieving and purse-cutting, also, being guilty of masterful bangstrie and oppression.' MacPherson was hanged at Banff Cross in 1700, and the story goes that he spent his last hours composing a defiant farewell Lament which he played en route to the gallows. In one version he offered the fiddle to anyone in the crowd who would take it, but since no one came forward, he smashed it over his knee; in another he destroyed the instrument at the gallows so that 'nae ither hand shall play on thee when I am dead and gone'. Burns probably knew the old ballad from a contemporary broadsheet and the tune (sometimes known as MacPherson's Rant) is found in Margaret Sinkler's MS of 1710 and the* Caledonian Pocket Companion *of 1755. 'Who except Burns', wrote Carlyle, 'could have given words to such a soul, words that we never listen to without a strange barbarous, half poetic feeling'. The original ballad was printed in a broadside entitled* MacPherson's Rant; or the last words of James McPherson, murderer *shortly after the events referred to, and consists of eleven eight-line stanzas 'in vigorous language of somewhat inferior rhyme': I spent my time in rioting,/ Debauch'd my health and strength;/ I pillag'd, plunder'd, murdered,/ But now, alas! at length// I'm brought to punishment condign;/ Pale death draws near to me,/ The end I never did project/ To die upon a tree.//*

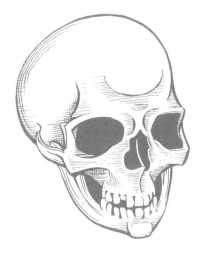

CHORUS AFTER EACH VERSE

A Highland lad my love was born,
The lalland laws he held in scorn,   *lowland*
But he still was faithfu' to his clan,
My gallant, braw John Highlandman!

Sing hey my braw John Highlandman!
Sing ho my braw John Highlandman!
There's not a lad in a' the lan'
Was match for my John Highlandman!

With his philabeg an' tartan plaid,   *kilt*
An' guid claymore down by his side,   *good large sword*
The ladies' hearts he did trepan,   *beguile*
My gallant, braw John Highlandman!

We ranged a' from Tweed to Spey,
An' liv'd like lords an' ladies gay;
For a lalland face he feared none, –
My gallant, braw John Highlandman.

They banish'd him beyond the sea,
But ere the bud was on the tree,
Adown my cheeks the pearls ran,
Embracing my John Highlandman!

But, och! they catch'd him at the last,
And bound him in a dungeon fast;
My curse upon them ev'ry one –
They've hang'd my braw John Highlandman!

And now a widow I must mourn
The pleasures that will ne'er return;
No comfort but a hearty can,
When I think on John Highlandman.

'A Highland lad' comes from Burns's cantata, Love and Liberty, *popularly known as* The Merry Beggars *since its posthumous publication in 1799. In the tradition of Gay's* Beggar's Opera, *recitatives link songs set to popular tunes. Burns was dissuaded from publishing it in the Edinburgh edition of his* Poems *because it was 'too licentious' and likely to damage his reputation. In the cantata 'A Highland lad' is sung by a drunk old robber woman.*

'The white cockade' was a Burns contribution to the Scots Musical Museum *(vol. III, no. 272): he slightly altered verses from Herd's folksong collection of 1776 to produce a Jacobite song – the White Cockade is a symbol of the House of Stewart. There are later variants. Burns set the verses to the tune 'O, an ye were dead, Guidman' from the* Caledonian Pocket Companion *of 1752. It is now mostly sung to the tune 'The White Cockade'.*

My love was born in Aberdeen,
The bonniest lad that e'er was seen,
But now he's made our hearts fu' sad,
He takes the field wi' his White Cockade.

O he's a ranting, roving lad,
He is a brisk an' a bonny lad.
Betide what may, I will be wed,
And follow the boy wi' the White Cockade.

I'll sell my rock, my tow, my reel,   *distaff/ flax*
My gude gray mare and hawkit cow   *white-faced*
To buy mysel a tartan plaid,
To follow the boy wi' the White Cockade.

O he's a ranting, roving lad,
He is a brisk an' a bonny lad.
Betide what may, I will be wed,
And follow the boy wi' the White Cockade.

Herd's version:

My love was born in Aberdeen,
The bonniest lad that e'er was seen;
O, he is forced from me to gae
Over the hills and far away!

O he's a ranting roving laddie
O he's a brisk and bonnie laddie
Betide what will, I'll get me ready
And follow the lad wi' the Highland plaidy.

I'll sell my rock, my reel, my tow,
My gude gray mare and hacket cow,
To buy my love a tartan plaid,
Because he is a roving blade. *[Chorus follows]*

About Yule, when the wind blew cool,
And the round tables began,
O, there is come to our king's court,
Mony a weel-favoured man.

The Queen looked o'er the castle wa',
Beheld baith dale and down,
And there she saw Young Waters
Come riding through the town.

His footmen they did rin before,
His horsemen rade behind;
And his mantle, of the burning gowd,   *gold*
Did keep him frae the wind.

Gowden-graithed his horse before,   *harnessed in gold*
And siller-shod behind;   *silver-shod*
The horse Young Waters rade upon
Was fleeter than the wind.

Out then spake a wily lord,
And to the queen said he;
'O, tell me, wha's the fairest face
Rides in the company?'

'I've seen lord, and I've seen laird,
And knight of high degree;
But a fairer face than Young Waters'
Mine een did never see.'

Out then spake the jealous king,
And an angry man was he;
'Oh, if he had been twice as fair,
You might have excepted me.'

'You're neither laird nor lord,' she says,
'But the king that wears the crown;
There is not a knight in fair Scotland,
But to thee maun bow down.'

For a' that she could do or say,
Appeased he wadna be;
And for the words which she had said,
Young Waters he maun dee.

They hae ta'en Young Waters,
Put fetters on his feet;
They hae ta'en Young Waters,
And thrown him in dungeon deep.

Aft I ha'e ridden through Stirling town,
In the wind both and the weet;
But I ne'er rade through Stirling town
Wi' fetters at my feet.

Aft hae I ridden through Stirling town,
In the wind both and the rain;
But I ne'er rade through Stirling town,
Ne'er to return again.

They ha'e ta'en to the Heading Hill,
His young son in his cradle;
And they ha'e ta'en to the Heading Hill
His horse both and his saddle.

They ha'e ta'en to the Heading Hill,
His lady fair to see;
And for the words the queen had spoke,
Young Waters he did dee.

Young Waters of this ballad is believed to have been Lord Walter, second son of Murdoch, Duke of Albany, who was executed along with his father, grandfather and brother in 1425 after the return of James I from captivity in England. Murdoch's incompetence as Regent had hastened Scotland's already severe financial and administrative disintegration and James found the authority of the Crown weakened, the power of the great nobles dangerously inflated, the administration chaotic, and 'poverty, lawlessness and pestilence abounding' (Fitzroy MacLean). He took drastic action against the house of Albany, and within a year Murdoch, his sons Walter and Alexander, and his octogenarian father-in-law, the Earl of Lennox, were seized, tried, convicted of a variety of crimes and beheaded at Stirling Castle. Their fate however aroused great sympathy among the common people who were impressed by their remarkably noble appearance. Similar tales of a king's fatal jealousy crop up in Scandinavian texts from the 16th century. (This text comes from Percy's Reliques of Ancient Poetry *and the tune from Eyre-Todd's* Ancient Scots Ballads *of 1894). 'Round tables': 'a peculiar, symmetrically shaped series of earthworks is still pointed out under the walls of Stirling Castle as the place where this now unknown game was wont to be played' (George Eyre-Todd).*

SIR PATRICK SPENCE

Moderate

con Ped.

The— king sits in Dun - ferm - ling toune, Drink - ing the blude reid wine: O—

quhair wull I gct a guid— sail - or, To— sail this schip of— mine?

Up and spak an eld - ern knicht, Sat at— the— king's richt kne: Sir

Pa - trick Spence is the best sail - or That sails— u - pon the se.

The King sits in Dunfermling toune,
Drinking the blude reid wine:
O quhair wull I get a guid sailor,
To sail this schip of mine?

Up and spak an eldern knicht,
Sat at the king's richt kne:
Sir PATRICK SPENCE is the best sailor
That sails upon the se.

The king has written a braid letter,
And signd it wi' his hand;
And sent it to Sir PATRICK SPENCE,
Was walking on the sand.

The first line that Sir PATRICK red,
A loud lauch lauched he:
The next line that Sir PATRICK red,
The teir blinded his ee.

O quha is this has done this deid,
This ill deid don to me;
To send me out this time o' the zeir,
To sail upon the se?

Mak haste, mak haste, my mirry men a,
Our guid schip sails the morne.
O say na sae, my master deir,
For I feir a deadlie storme.

Late late yestreen I saw the new moone,
Wi' the auld moone in hir arme;
And I feir, my dear master ,
That we wull cum to harme.

O our Scotch nobles wer richt laith
To weet thair cork-heild shoone;
Bot, lang or a' the play were playd,
They wat thair heads aboone.

O lang, lang, may thair ladies sit
Wi' their fans into thair hand,
Or eir they se Sir PATRICK SPENCE
Cum sailing to the land.

O lang, lang may thair ladies stand
Wi' thair gold kems in their hair,
Waiting for thair ain deir lordes,
For they'll se thame na mair.

Haff owre, haff owre to Aberdour,
It's fiftie fadom deip:
And thair lies guid Sir PATRICK SPENCE,
Wi' the Scots Lordes at his feit.

This version of the old ballad 'Sir Patrick Spens' comes from Herd's Ancient & Modern Scots Songs *(1776) and the tune from* Albyn's Anthology *of 1818. Popularly, the ballad referred to the home-bringing of Margaret, 'Maid of Norway', who was declared Queen of Scotland in 1286 at the age of three, and who died in Orkney in 1290, without ever having set foot on the Scottish mainland. It may refer, though, to the shipwreck, on their return home, of the Scots nobles who conveyed the Maid's mother, Margaret, daughter of Alexander III, to her marriage with Eric of Norway in 1281. Lady Wardlaw's name has been associated with 'Sir Patrick Spens' but there is no hard evidence that she was the author. This Fife-born poet (1677–1727) published 'Hardyknute' in 1719, claiming that it was the fragment of an ancient ballad found in a vault in Dunfermline, but it was subsequently suggested that it was her own work, based on 'Gilderoy'.*

FINE FLOWERS IN THE VALLEY *Traditional*

She sat down below a thorn,
Fine flowers in the valley,
And there she has her sweet babe born,
And the green leaves they grow rarely.

Smile na sae sweet, my bonnie babe
Fine flowers in the valley,
And ye smile sae sweet, ye'll smile me dead,
And the green leaves they grow rarely.

She's taen out her little penknife
Fine flowers in the valley,
And twinn'd the sweet babe o' its life,   *deprived*
And the green leaves they grow rarely.

She's howket a grave by the light o' the moon,   *dug*
Fine flowers in the valley,
And there she's buried her sweet babe in,
And the green leaves they grow rarely.

As she was going to the church,
Fine flowers in the valley,
She saw a sweet babe in the porch,
And the green leaves they grow rarely.

O sweet babe and thou were mine,
Fine flowers in the valley,
I wad cleed thee in the silk so fine,
And the green leaves they grow rarely.

O mither dear, when I was thine,
Fine flowers in the valley,
You did na prove to me sae kind,
And the green leaves they grow rarely.

Later versions of this 17th-century broadside, e.g. 'The Cruel Mother', crop up in Britain, Canada and the United States. Concealed pregnancy and infanticide are common themes in Scottish ballads (see 'The Four Maries'). Burns gave the song to the Scots Musical Museum (1792, vol. IV, no. 320).

LOVE SATISFIED

There's nought but care on ev-'ry han', In ev-'ry hour that pas-ses, O: What

sig-ni-fies the life o' man, An' 'twere na for the las-ses, O. *Green grow the rash-es, O;*

Green grow the rash-es, O; The sweet-est hours that e'er I spend, Are spent a-mang the las-ses, O.

CHORUS AFTER EACH VERSE

There's nought but care on ev'ry han',   *hand*
In ev'ry hour that passes, O:
What signifies the life o' man,
An' 'twere na for the lasses, O.

Green grow the rashes, O;
Green grow the rashes, O;
The sweetest hours that e'er I spend,
Are spent amang the lasses, O.

The warly race may riches chase,   *worldly*
An' riches still may fly them, O;
An' tho' at last they catch them fast,
Their hearts can ne'er enjoy them, O.

But gie me a canny hour at e'en,   *favourable*
My arms about my Dearie, O;
An' warly cares, an' warly men,
May a' gae tapsalteerie, O.   *topsy-turvy*

For you sae douse, ye sneer at this,   *so sedate*
Ye're nought but senseless asses, O:
The wisest Man the warl' saw,   *Solomon*
He dearly lov'd the lasses, O.

Auld Nature swears, the lovely Dears
Her noblest work she classes, O:
Her prentice han' she try'd on man,
An' then she made the lasses, O.

Green grow the rashes, O;
Green grow the rashes, O;
The sweetest hours that e'er I spend,
Are spent amang the lasses, O.

This great favourite was the first of Burns's songs to be printed – with the music – in the Scots Musical Museum, *1787 (vol. I, no. 77). It appears – minus the last verse – in* The Commonplace Book, *dated August 1784. Here the poet had classified young men in two categories or 'grand Classes' – the Grave and the Merry, and he quoted this song as an example: '. . . I shall set down the following fragment which, as it is the genuine language of my heart, will enable any body to determine which of the Classes I belong to – Green grow the rashes – O.' On 3 September, 1786, Burns sent the less delicate version to his friend, John Richmond, with a note announcing the birth of twins to Jean Armour: 'Wish me luck . . . Armour has just now brought me a fine boy and a girl at one throw. God bless the poor little dears!' A version of the tune occurs in Straloch's MS (1627) and it is in many 18th-century collections.*

CHORUS AFTER EACH VERSE

Green grow the rashes O,
Green grow the rashes O,
The lasses they hae wimble bores   *have gimlet holes*
The widows they hae gashes O.

In sober hours I am a priest;
A hero when I'm tipsey, O;
But I'm a king and ev'ry thing
When wi' a wanton Gipsey, O.

'Twas late yestreen I met wi' ane,
An' wow, but she was gentle, O!
Ae han' she pat roun' my cravat,   *one hand*
The tither to my p – – e, O.   *pintle*

I dought na speak – yet was na fley'd –   *daren't/ scared*
My heart play'd duntie, duntie, O;   *thumpety-thump*
An' ceremony laid aside,
I fairly fun' her c—ntie, O.–   *found*

Green grow the rashes O,
Green grow the rashes O,
The lasses they hae wimble bores
The widows they hae gashes O.

AS I CAME O'ER THE CAIRNEY MOUNT

As I came o'er the Cairney mount, And down amang the bloom-ing hea-ther, Kind-ly stood the milk-ing-shiel To shel-ter frae the storm-y wea-ther. O, my bon-nie High-land lad, My win-some, weel-far'd High-land lad-die! Wha wad mind the

wind and rain Sae weel ro'd in his tar-tan plaid - ie!

CHORUS AFTER EACH VERSE

As I came o'er the Cairney mount,
And down amang the blooming heather,
Kindly stood the milking-shiel   *milking-shed*
To shelter frae the stormy weather.

O, my bonnie Highland lad,
My winsome, weelfar'd Highland laddie!
Wha wad mind the wind and rain
Sae weel ro'd in his tartan plaidie!   *well wrapped*

Now Phoebus blinkit on the bent,   *gleamed/ moor*
And o'er the knowes the lambs were bleating:
But he wan my heart's consent,
To be his ain at the neist meeting. –   *next*

Apart from being an inspired songwriter, Robert Burns was a folksong collector
in the modern sense, who faithfully recorded both words and melodies of
traditional songs wherever he found them. If only a melody existed, or a mere
fragment of verse or chorus, he would complete it with words fitting the
character and mood of the music. He also altered and 'improved' traditional
material, substituting polite words for those of obscene traditional songs, to
make them fit for mixed company. This one, like 'The Birks of Aberfeldy', is
a case in point: 'The first and indeed most beautiful set of this tune', wrote Burns,
'was formerly, and in some places is still known by the name of "As I cam o'er
the Cairney Mount", which is the first line of an excellent, but somewhat
licentious song still sung to the tune.' The melody (entitled 'The highland lassie')
was first printed in Oswald's Curious Collection of Scots Tunes *in 1740 and*
is also in the Caledonian Pocket Companion *of 1743. Burns's version was*
published in the Scots Musical Museum *of 1796 (vol. V, no. 467).*

As I cam o'er the Cairney mount
And down amang the blooming heather,
The Highland laddie drew his durk
And sheath'd it in my wanton leather.

O my bonnie, bonnie Highland lad,
My handsome, charming Highland laddie;
When I am sick and like to die,
He'll row me in his Highland plaidie.

With me he play'd his warlike pranks,
And on me boldly did adventure,
He did attack me on both flanks,
And pushed me fiercely in the centre.

A furious battle then began,
Wi' equal courage and desire,
Altho' he stuck me three to one,
I stood my ground and receiv'd his fire.

But our ammunition being spent,
And we quite out of breath an' sweating,
We did agree with ae consent,
To fight it out at our next meeting.

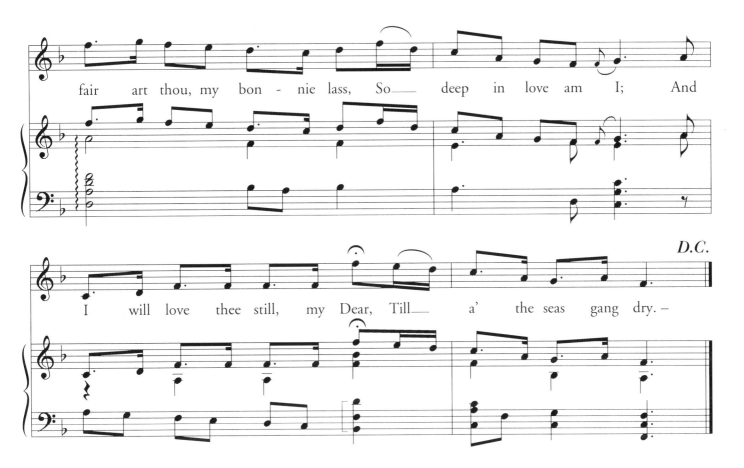

fair art thou, my bon - nie lass, So— deep in love am I; And

D.C.

I will love thee still, my Dear, Till— a' the seas gang dry. –

O my Luve's like a red, red rose,
That's newly sprung in June;
O my luve's like the melodie
That's sweetly play'd in tune.

As fair art thou, my bonnie lass,
So deep in love am I;
And I will love thee still, my Dear,
Till a' the seas gang dry. –

Till a' the seas gang dry, my Dear,
And the rocks melt wi' the sun:
O I will love thee still, my Dear,
While the sands o' life shall run. –

And fare thee weel, my only Love!
O fare thee weel a while!
And I will come again, my Luve,
Tho' it were ten thousand mile!

This is probably Burns's most famous love song. He took it down from the singing of a country girl and altered and extended it to form 'one of the world's most perfect lyrics'. Nowadays it is more often sung to a variation of 'Low down in the broom' from Oswald's Caledonian Pocket Companion *of c.1754, but this one, 'Major Graham', is the tune Burns contributed to the* Scots Musical Museum *of 1796 (vol. V, no. 402). It features in both Niel Gow's* Strathspeys *(1784) and Aird's* Airs *of 1788.*

GRADH GEAL MO CHRIDH *Gaelic*

Bheir mi ò - ro bhan ó Bheir mi ò - ro bhan ì Bheir mi

ò - ru o hó 'S mi tha bròn - ach's tu'm dhìth. 'S iom-adh

oidh - che fliuch is fuar Ghabh mi cuairt is mi leam fhìn Gus an

d'ràin - ig mi'n t-àit Far'n robh gràdh geal mo chrìdh.

Bheir mi òro bhan ó
Bheir mi òro bhan ì
Bheir mi òru o hò
'S mi tha brònach 's tu'm dhìth.

'S iomadh oidhche fliuch is fuar
Ghabh mi cuairt is mi leam fhìn
Gus an d'ràinig mi'n t-àit
Far'n robh gràdh geal mo chrìdh.

Bheir mi òro bhan ó
Bheir mi òro bhan ì
Bheir mi òru o hò
'S mi tha brònach 's tu'm dhìth.

Vair mi oro van o
Vair mi oro van ee
Vair mi oru o ho
Sad am I without thee.

When I'm lonely dear white heart
Black the night or wild the sea,
By love's light my foot finds
The old pathway to thee.

Vair mi oro van o
Vair mi oro van ee
Vair mi oru o ho
Sad am I without thee.

In her search for fresh material, the folksong collector Marjory Kennedy-Fraser went to the remote little isle of Eriskay, between Barra and South Uist: 'a mere gull's nest, scarcely worth the name of an island, storm-beaten, windswept, treeless, shelterless, rocky . . .' This song was taken down from the singing of Mary MacInnes and since its publication in Kennedy-Fraser's Songs of the Hebrides *in 1909, it has become a firm favourite. Incidentally, Eriskay was where Bonnie Prince Charlie and seven supporters first landed in Britain on July 23, 1745. It was also the island off which the merchant ship* S.S. Politician *sank in 1941 carrying a precious cargo of 20,000 cases of whisky which were unofficially salvaged by the locals – the basis of Sir Compton Mackenzie's novel* Whisky Galore.

FLOW GENTLY, SWEET AFTON

Moderate

con Ped.

Flow gen-tly, sweet_ Af-ton, a-mong thy green_ braes, Flow

gen-tly, I'll _ sing_ thee a _ song in_ thy_ praise; My_

Ma-ry's_ a-sleep by thy mur-mur-ing_ stream,_ Flow

gen-tly, sweet_ Af-ton, dis-turb not_ her_ dream!

Flow gently, sweet Afton, among thy green braes,
Flow gently, I'll sing thee a song in thy praise;
My Mary's asleep by thy murmuring stream,
Flow gently, sweet Afton, disturb not her dream!

Thou stock-dove whose echo resounds thro' the glen,
Ye wild whistling blackbirds in yon thorny den,
Thou green-crested lapwing thy screaming forbear,
I charge you, disturb not my slumbering fair.

How lofty, sweet Afton, thy neighbouring hills,
Far mark'd with the courses of clear, winding rills;
There daily I wander as noon rises high,
My flocks and my Mary's sweet cot in my eye.

How pleasant thy banks and green vallies below,
Where wild in the woodlands the primroses blow;
There oft, as mild ev'ning weeps over the lea,
The sweet-scented birk shades my Mary and me.

Thy crystal stream, Afton, how lovely it glides,
And winds by the cot where my Mary resides;
How wanton thy waters her snowy feet lave,
As gathering sweet flow'rets she stems thy clear wave.

Flow gently, sweet Afton, among thy green braes,
Flow gently, sweet river, the theme of my lays;
My Mary's asleep by thy murmuring stream,
Flow gently, sweet Afton, disturb not her dream!

'There is a small river, Afton', wrote Burns to Mrs Dunlop in 1789, 'that falls into Nith, near New Cumnock, which has some charming, wild, romantic scenery on its banks. – I have a particular pleasure in those little pieces of poetry such as our Scots songs, &c. where the names and landskip – features of rivers, lakes, or woodlands, that one knows, are introduced. – I attempted a compliment of that kind, to Afton . . .' The song was included in the Scots Musical Museum *(vol. IV, no. 386) and the poet's brother believed that it was addressed to Mary Campbell or 'Highland Mary'. The tune is 'Afton Water'.*

CHORUS AFTER EACH VERSE

It was in and through the window broads   *shutters*
And a' the tirliewirlies o't,   *latticework*
The sweetest kiss that e'er I got
Was from my dainty Davie.

Oh, leeze me on your curly pow,   I'm very fond of.../ head
Dainty Davie, dainty Davie,
Leeze me on your curly pow,
My ain dear dainty Davie.

It was doon amang my daddy's pease,
And underneath the cherry-trees –
Oh, there he kist me as he pleased,
For he was my ain Davie.

When he was chased by a dragoon,
Into my bed he was laid doon.
I thocht him worthy o' his room,
For he's aye my dainty Davie.

Oh, leeze me on your curly pow,
Dainty Davie, dainty Davie,
Leeze me on your curly pow,
My ain dear dainty Davie.

Being pursu'd by the dragoons,
Within my bed he was laid down
And weel I wat he was worth his room,
My ain dear dainty Davie.

O leeze me on his curly pow,
Bonnie Davie, dainty Davie;
Leeze me on his curly pow,
He was my dainty Davie.

My minnie laid him at my back,
I trow he lay na lang at that,
But turn'd, and in a verra crack
Produc'd a dainty Davie.

Then in the field amang the pease
Behin' the house o' Cherrytrees,
Again he wan atweesh my thies
And, splash! gaed out his gravy.

But had I goud, or had I land,
It should be a' at his command;
I'll ne'er forget what he pat i' my hand,
It was a dainty Davie.

O leeze me on his curly pou
Bonnie Davie, dainty Davi
Leeze me on his curly pow,
He was my dainty Davie.

The original 'Dainty Davie' (from Herd's collection of 1776) was reputedly the Rev. David Williamson (died 1706) who was obliged, on account of his allegiance to the Solemn League and Covenant, to seek refuge from the dragoons at the home of the Laird of Cherrytrees. Lady Cherrytree hid him in her daughter's bed with foreseeable consequences and the two ended up married. Burns was more explicit in his version of the Herd song which comes from his private collection of bawdy songs, the Merry Muses of Caledonia, *published in 1959. Burns set words to the traditional tune 'Dainty Davie' on no less than three occasions: 'There was a lad was born in Kyle' (1787), 'Meet me on the warlock knowe' (1793) and 'Lovely was she by the dawn' (1794) – this last in order to supply publisher George Thomson with more English songs for his collection.*

Corn___ rigs,___ an' bar - ley rigs, An'___ corn___ rigs___ are___ bon - ny: I'll

ne'er for - get___ that___ hap - py___ night,___ A - mang_ the___ rigs___ wi'___ An - nie.

It was upon a Lammas night,	*harvest*
When corn rigs are bonny,	*ridges*
Beneath the moon's unclouded light	
I held awa to Annie:	
The time flew by, wi' tentless heed,	*careless*
Till 'tween the late and early,	
Wi' sma' persuasions she agreed,	
To see me thro' the barley.	

Corn rigs, an' barley rigs,
An' corn rigs are bonny:
I'll ne'er forget that happy night,
Amang the rigs wi' Annie.

The sky was blue, the wind was still,
The moon was shining clearly;
I set her down, wi' right good will,
Amang the rigs o' barley:
I kent her heart was a' my ain;
I lov'd her most sincerely;
I kiss'd her owre and owre again,
Amang the rigs o' barley.

Corn rigs, an' barley rigs,
An' corn rigs are bonny:
I'll ne'er forget that happy night,
Amang the rigs wi' Annie.

I lock'd her in my fond embrace;
Her heart was beating rarely:
My blessings on that happy place,
Amang the rigs o' barley!
But by the moon and stars so bright,
That shone that night so clearly!
She ay shall bless that happy night,
Amang the rigs o' barley.

Corn rigs, an' barley rigs,
An' corn rigs are bonny:
I'll ne'er forget that happy night,
Amang the rigs wi' Annie.

I hae been blythe wi' Comrades dear;
I hae been merry drinking;
I hae been joyfu' gath'rin gear;   *goods, property*
I hae been happy thinking;
But a' the pleasures e'er I saw,
Tho' three times doubl'd fairly,
That happy night was worth them a',
Amang the rigs o' barley.

Corn rigs, an' barley rigs,
An' corn rigs are bonny:
I'll ne'er forget that happy night,
Amang the rigs wi' Annie.

Several girls claimed to be the original 'Annie' of Burns's song and while no one can be quite sure who she was, it is thought that the girl who romped in the corn with the poet was the daughter of one of his neighbours, a farmer called Rankine. Burns was proud of this early composition based on an old fragment ('O corn rigs and rye rigs,/ O corn rigs is bonnie;/ Whare'er you meet a bonnie lass,/ Preen up her apron, Johnie.') and it is one of his most popular songs. The tune occurs in various 18th-century collections and has Ramsay's words in Orpheus Caledonius *(vol. II, no. 18) and the* Scots Musical Museum *(vol. I, no. 93). Allan Ramsay (1684–1758) was born in Leadhills but came to Edinburgh in 1700 to be apprenticed to a wigmaker. He later became a bookseller, publisher, author, theatrical impresario, auctioneer and dealer in decorative art. He played an important part in preserving and handing on the heritage of earlier Scots poetry at a time*

when, shortly after the union of parliaments in 1705, he and many other Scots felt their culture in danger of Anglicization: a fear that has persisted ever since. The five volumes of his Tea-Table Miscellany *(1724–37) brought together many traditional Scottish songs and ballads, to which he added compositions of his own. The following specimen is stilted compared with Burns's version, but Ramsay's example made it easier for Burns to become the genius he was.*

My *Patie* is a Lover gay,
His Mind is never muddy,
His Breath is sweeter than new Hay,
His Face is fair and ruddy.
His Shape is handsome, middle Size,
He's stately in his wawking:
The shining of his Een surprise;
'Tis Heaven to hear him tawking.

Last Night I met him on a Bawk,   *ridge*
Where yellow Corn was growing,
There mony a kindly Word he spake,
That set my Heart a glowing.
He kiss'd, and vow'd he wad be mine,
And loo'd me best of ony;
That gars me like to sing sinsyne,   *makes/ since then*
O Corn Riggs are bonny.

Let Maidens of a silly Mind,
Refuse what maist they're wanting,
Since we for yielding are design'd,
We chastly should be granting:
Then I'll comply, and marry *Pate,*
And syne my Cockernony,   *and from then my hair [style]*
He's free to touzle air or late,   *early*
Where Corn Riggs are bonny.

LOVE
DOOMED
OR REJECTED

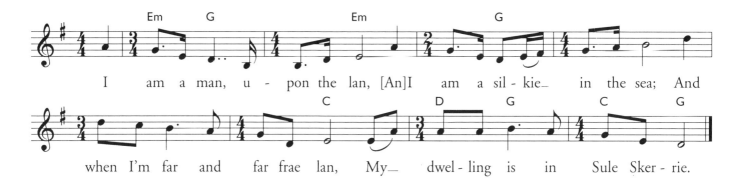

I am a man, u-pon the lan, [An]I am a sil-kie in the sea; And when I'm far and far frae lan, My dwel-ling is in Sule Sker-rie.

An eartly nourris sits and sings,   *nurse*
And aye she sings, Ba, lily wean!
Little ken I my bairnis father,
Far less the land that he staps in.

Then ane arose at her bed-fit,
An a grumly guest I'm sure was he: *gloomy*
'Here am I, thy bairnis father,
Although that I be not comelie.

I am a man, upon the lan,
An I am a silkie in the sea;
And when I'm far and far frae lan,
My dwelling is in Sule Skerrie.'

'It was na weel,' quo the maiden fair,
'It was na weel, indeed,' quo she,
'That the Great Silkie of Sule Skerrie
Suld hae come and aught a bairn to me.'   *begot a child on*

Now he has taen a purse o' goud,
And he has pat it upo her knee,
Sayin, 'Gie to me my little young son,
An tak thee up thy nourris-fee.

'An it sall come to pass on a simmer's day,
When the sin shines het on evera stane,
That I will tak my little young son,
An teach him for to swim the faem.   *foam*

'An thu sall marry a proud gunner,
An a proud gunner I'm sure he'll be,
An the very first schot that ere he schoots,
He'll schoot baith my young son and me.'

Sule Skerry is a remote island to the west of Orkney. Silkies or selchies were believed to be seals able to cast their skins and assume human form on land. The theme of the silkie man or woman marrying a human is a common one in folk tales of North and West Scotland, and the often fruitful union is invariably achieved by trickery. Sometimes the silkie is prevented from returning to sea because the human spouse has hidden his or her seal skin. The Orkney ballad above was first spotted in the Proceedings of The Scottish Society of Antiquaries *for 1852 by William Macmath, who was a friend and collaborator of the great ballad collector, Child. 'It was communicated,' said Macmath, 'by the late Captain F. W. L. Thomas, R. N.; written down by him from the dictation of a venerable lady of Snarra Voe, Shetland.' The version following was rediscovered by a Scandinavian folksong specialist, Dr Otto Andersson, who heard the fifth stanza sung by John Sinclair in the island of of Flotta in Orkney in 1938.*

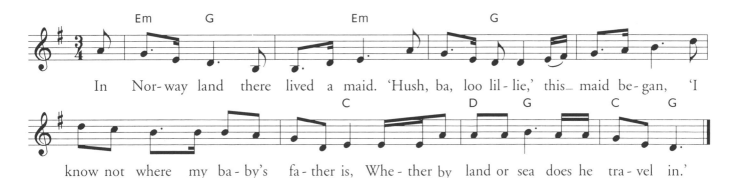

In Norway land there lived a maid.
'Hush, ba, loo lillie,' this maid began,
'I know not where my baby's father is,
Whether by land or sea does he travel in.'

It happened on a certain day,
When this fair lady fell asleep,
That in cam' a good grey selchie
And set him down at her bed feet.

Saying 'Awak', awak' my pretty fair maid,
For oh, how sound as thou dost sleep,
An' I'll tell thee where thy baby's father is,
He's sittin' close at thy bed feet.'

'I pray come tell to me thy name,
Oh, tell me where does thy dwelling be?'
'My name is good Hein Mailer,
I earn my livin' oot o' the sea.'

'I am a man upon the land,
I am a selchie in the sea,
An' whin I'm far from every strand,
My dwelling is in Shool Skerry.'

'Alas, alas this woeful fate,
This weary fate that's been laid on me,
That a man should come from the Wast o' Hoy
To the Norway lands to have a bairn wi' me.'

'My dear, I'll wed thee with a ring,
With a ring, my dear, will I wed with thee.
Thoo may go wed thee weddens wi' whom thoo wilt,
For I'm sure thoo'll never wed none wi' me.'

'Thoo will nurse my little wee son
For seven long years upon thy knee;
An' at the end o' seven long years
I'll come back and pay the nursing fee.'

She's nursed her little wee son
For seven long years upon her knee;
An' at the en o' seven long years
He came back wi' gold and white monie.

He says, 'My dear, I'll wed thee wi' ring,
Wi' a ring, my dear, I'll wed wi' thee.
Thoo mat go wed thee weddens wi' whom thoo wilt,
For I'm sure thoo'll never wed none wi' me.'

'But I'll put a gold chain around his neck,
An' a gey good gold chain it'll be,
That if ever he comes to the Norway lands,
Thoo may bae a gey good guess on he.

'An thoo will get a gunner good,
An' a gey good gunner it will be,
An' he'll go out a May morning
An shoot the son an' the grey selchie.'

Oh, she has got a gunner good,
An' a gey good gunner it was he,
An' he gaed oot on a May morning
An' he shot the son an' the grey selchie.

'Alas, alas, this woeful fate,
This weary fate that's been laid on me,'
An' ance or twice she sobbed and sighed,
An' her tender heart did brak in three.

Slow

con Ped.

I've heard them lilt - ing at our___ yowe - milk - ing,

Lass - es a' - lilt - in' be - fore the dawn o' day; But now___ they are moan - ing on

il - ka green___ loan - ing,—The Flowers of the For - est are a' wede a - way.

I've heard them lilting at our yowe-milking,   *ewe-*
Lasses a'liltin' before the dawn o' day;   *girls singing*
But now they are moaning on ilka green loaning, –
The Flowers of the Forest are a' wede away.   *taken away*

At buchts, in the morning,   *sheepfolds*
    nae blythe lads are scorning,
The lasses are lonely and dowie, and wae;   *sad*
Nae daffin, nae gabbin',   *no fun, no chatting*
    but sighing and sabbing,
Ilk ane lifts her leglen and hies her away.   *milkpail*

In hairst, at the shearing,   *harvest*
    nae youths now are jeering,
The bandsters are lyart,   *sheave-binders/ grizzled*
    and runkled and grey;   *wrinkled*
At fair, or at preaching,
    nae wooing, nae fleeching –   *flattery*
The Flowers of the Forest are a' wede away.

At e'en in the gloaming, nae swankies are roaming
'Bout stacks wi' the lasses at bogle to play;   *hide-and-seek*
But ilk ane sits drearie, lamenting her dearie, –
The Flowers of the Forest are a' wede away.

Dule and wae for the order   *grief and woe*
    sent our lads to the Border!
The English, for ance, by guile wan the day;
The Flowers of the Forest,
    that foucht aye the foremost, –
The prime o' our land, are cauld in the clay.

We'll hear nae mair lilting at the yowe-milking,
Women and bairns are heartless and wae;
Sighing and moaning on ilka green loaning, –   *track*
The Flowers of the Forest are a' wede away.

The version above refers to the battle of Flodden (September, 1513)
where King James IV and his army were wiped out by Henry VIII's
troops. Every farm and household in lowland Scotland was affected
by the slaughter. The 'Flowers' of the song were the Scottish losses and
the 'Forest', Ettrick Forest, west of Selkirk. Jean Elliot, a reserved and
studious spinster (1727–1805) used the first two lines of the old song
when her brother challenged her to write a new ballad of Flodden

Field in 1756. Alison Rutherford (1713–97) was wife of Lord
Cockburn, Edinburgh advocate, and her drawing-room became a
literary salon. She recognized the genius of young Walter Scott and
wrote of Burns:'The town is at present agog with the ploughman
poet', she wrote, 'who receives adulation with native dignity, and is
the very figure of his profession, strong and coarse, but has a most
enthusiastic heart of love'. Burns wrote to his publisher: "The Flowers
of the Forest" is charming as a poem; & should be & must be, set to
the notes; but though out of your rule, the three Stanzas beginning,
"I hae seen the smiling o' Fortune beguiling", are worthy of a place,
were it but to immortalise the Author of them, who is an old lady of
my acquaintance . . .' Her version refers to the ruin of noble
Border families by unwise investment during the 18th century. The
tune is in the 17th-century Skene manuscript and in Johnson's Scots
Musical Museum of 1787 (vol. I, no. 63). There is a version for
bagpipes.

I've seen the smiling
    Of Fortune beguiling;
I've felt all its favours, and found its decay;
Sweet was its blessing,
    Kind its caressing,
But now it is fled – fled far away!

I've seen the forest
    Adorned the foremost,
With flowers of the fairest, most pleasant and gay;
Sae bonnie was their blooming!
    Their scent the air perfuming!
But now they are withered and a' wede away.

I've seen the morning
    With gold the hills adorning,
And loud tempests storming before the mid-day;
I've seen Tweed's silver streams
    Glittering in the sunny beams
Grow drumly and dark as they rolled on their way.   *muddy*

Oh, fickle Fortune!
    Why this cruel sporting?
Why thus perplex us, poor sons of a day?
Nae mair your smiles can cheer me,
    Nae mair your frowns can fear me,
For the Flowers of the Forest are a' wede away.

Lively

Gil - de - roy__ was a bon - ny__ Boy, When he came to__ the__ Glen, With

sil - ken Stock - ings__ on his__ Legs, And Ro - ses on__ his__ Shoon: He__

was a come - ly__ Sight__ to__ see, My__ Dear, and on - ly__ Joy; But__

now__ he__ hangs__ high__ on a__ Tree, My__ poor, pale Gil - de - roy.

Gilderoy was a bonny Boy,
When he came to the Glen,
With silken Stockings on his Legs,
And Roses on his Shoon:
He was a comely Sight to see,
My Dear, and only Joy;
But now he hangs high on a Tree,
My poor, pale *Gilderoy.*

Gilderoy was as brave a Man,
As ever *Scotland* bred;
Descended from a *Highland* Clan,
But a Caper till his Trade.   *brigand*
Our Fathers and our Mothers baith
Of us they had great Joy;
Expecting still the Wedding-Day,
'Tween me and *Gilderoy.*

When *Gilderoy* went to the Glen,
He always choos'd the Fat;
And in these days there were not ten,
With him durst bell the Cat:
For had he been as *Walace* stout,
And tall as *Dalmahoy,*
He never mist to get a Clout,
Frae my love *Gilderoy.*

The Queen of *Scots* possessed nought,
That my Love let me want;
For Cow and Ew he brought to me,
And e'en when they were scant:
All these did honestly possess,
He never did annoy,
Who never fail'd to pay their Cess *blackmail*
To my love *Gilderoy.*

But ah! they catch'd him on a Hill,
And baith his Hands they tied;
Alledging he had done much ill;
But Sons of Whores they lyed:
Three gallons large of Usquebaugh, *whisky*
We drank to his last Foy, *farewell feast*
Before he went to *Edinburgh,*
My dearest *Gilderoy.*

To *Edinburgh* I followed fast;
But long e'er I came there,
They had him mounted on a Mast,
And wagging in the Air.
His Relicks there were mair esteem'd,
Than *Scanderbeg* and *Croy;*
And ev'ry man was happy deem'd,
That gaz'd on *Gilderoy.*

Alas! that e'er such Laws were made,
To hang a Man for Gear;
Either for stealing Cow or Sheep,
Or yet for Horse or Mare:
Had not the Laws then been so strict,
I had never lost my Joy;
But now he lodges with auld *Nick,*
That hang'd my *Gilderoy.*

Yet another ballad about the life and execution of a highland rogue related by an ardent admirer, but too good a one to omit. A version of this ballad was published as a broadsheet about 1650, and this one comes from William Thomson's Orpheus Caledonius *of 1733 (vol. II, no. 47). Gilderoy, or Gille Ruadh (the Red-Haired Man), was Patrick Macgregor, leader of a band of violent robbers who terrorized the Highlands of Perthshire around the beginning of the 17th century. The Stewarts of Athole offered a reward of a thousand pounds for his apprehension and he was captured, tried and condemned to death with seven of his accomplices in February, 1636. At his execution at Edinburgh Cross in July, 1636, he received the doubtful distinction of a higher gibbet than the others – which is alluded to in some versions of the ballad, e.g. that in D'Urfey's* Pills to Purge Melancholy *of 1790:*

> They hung him high abune the rest,
> He was sae trim a boy;
> There died the youth whom I loved best,
> My handsome Gilderoy.

Lady Wardlaw (1677–1727), authoress of the ballad 'Hardyknute', is believed to have had a hand in the D'Urfey version, and its original was said to have contained 'some indecent luxuriances that required the pruning-hook'. Note: Scanderbeg, otherwise known as Iskander Bey, was a Turkish general who rejected Islam and, with slight help from Venice and the pope, ruled Albania as an independant nation until his death in 1468. I don't know who Croy was.

BONNY BARBARA ALLAN

Moderate

It was in and a-bout the Mar-tin-mas time, When the green leaves were a fall-ing, That Sir John Graham, in the west coun-trie, Fell in love with Bar-bara Al-lan.

con Ped.

It was in and about the Martinmas time,
When the green leaves were a falling,
That Sir John Graham, in the west countrie,
Fell in love with Barbara Allan.

He sent his man down thro' the town,
To the place where she was dwelling;
O haste and come to my master dear,
Gin ye be Barbara Allan.

O hooly hooly rose she up,   *slowly slowly*
To the place where he was lying,
And when she drew the curtin by,
Young man, I think you're dying.

O it's I'm sick, and very, very sick,
And 'tis a' for Barbara Allan.
O the better for me ye's never be,
Tho' your heart's blood were a spilling.

O dinna ye mind, young man, said she,
When ye the cups was fillin
That ye made the healths gae round and round,
And slighted Barbara Allan?

He turn'd his face unto the wa',
And death was with him dealing,
Adieu, adieu, my dear friends a',
And be kind to Barbara Allan.

And slowly, slowly raise she up,
And slowly, slowly left him,
And sighing, said, she could not stay,
Since death of life had reft him.

She had nae gane a mile but twa,
When she heard the deid-bell knelling,
And ev'ry jow that the deid-bell geid,   *stroke*
It cry'd, woe to Barbara Allan!

O mother, mother, mak my bed,
O make it saft and narrow;
Since my love died for me today,
I'll die for him tomorrow.

There are around two hundred tune versions of this enduringly popular old ballad and they are found on both sides of the Scottish border as well as across the Atlantic. Pepys mentions hearing an actress singing 'the little Scotch song of Barbery Allen' in his Diary of January 2, 1666, but this is the earliest printed Scottish text, from Allan Ramsay's Tea-Table Miscellany *of c. 1724, which Johnson published with the old Scottish tune in the* Scots Musical Museum *(vol. III, no. 221). According to tradition, the location of the story is Annan in Dumfriesshire, in which case the hero (if such he can be called) would have been one of the Grahams of the* Debatable Land, *who were prominent in the continual Border fighting of the fifteenth and sixteenth centuries. (Debatable Land:* land subject to dispute; the land on the Scottish–English border, especially between the Esk and the Sark.)

Slow

The— win-ter it is past, and the sum-mer's come at last, And the

con Ped.

small birds sing on ev' - ry— tree:——— The— hearts of these are

glad, but— mine is ve-ry sad, For my lo-ver has part-ed from me.

The winter it is past, and the summer's come at last,
And the small birds sing on ev'ry tree:
The hearts of these are glad,
        but mine is very sad,
For my lover has parted from me.

The rose upon the brier, by the waters running clear,
May have charms for the linnet or the bee;
Their little loves are blest
        and their little hearts at rest,
But my lover is parted from me.

My love is like the sun, in the firmament does run,
Forever is constant and true;
But his is like the moon
        that wanders up and down,
And every month it is new.

All you that are in love and cannot it remove,
I pity the pains you endure:
For experience makes me know
        that your hearts are full of woe,
A woe that no mortal can cure.

Burns revised a popular stall-ballad ('The lovesick maid') for this contribution to Johnson's Scots Musical Museum *of 1792 (vol. II, no. 200). He added a completely new second stanza and omitted two weak ones referring to the original subject of the song, a highwayman called Johnson who was hanged in 1750 for robbery in the Curragh of Kildare. The result is a timeless and universal love song. The tune, 'The winter it is past', is in the* Caledonian Pocket Companion *(Vol. X, 1759).*

With feeling, expressive

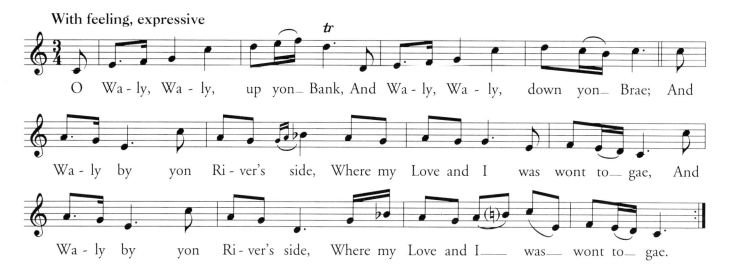

O Wa-ly, Wa-ly, up yon_ Bank, And Wa-ly, Wa-ly, down yon_ Brae; And

Wa-ly by yon Ri-ver's side, Where my Love and I was wont to_ gae, And

Wa-ly by yon Ri-ver's side, Where my Love and I___ was__ wont to_ gae.

O Waly, Waly, up yon Bank,   *Alas, Alas*
And Waly, Waly, down yon Brae;
And Waly by yon River's side,
Where my Love and I was wont to gae.

Waly, Waly, gin Love be bonny,
A little while when it is new;
But when it's auld, it waxes cauld
And wears away, like Morning Dew.

I leant my Back unto an Aik,   *oak*
I thought it was a trusty Tree;
But first it bow'd, and sine it brake,   *then*
And sae did my fause Love to me.   *false*

When Cockle-shells turn siller Bells,
And Muscles grow on ev'ry Tree;
When Frost and Snaw shall warm us a',
Then shall my Love prove true to me.

Now *Arthur-Seat* shall be my Bed,
The Sheets shall ne'er be fyl'd by me;   *defiled*
Saint *Anton's* Well shall be my Drink,
Since my true Love has forsaken me.

O *Martinmas* wind, when wilt thou blaw,
And shake the green Leaves off the Tree?
O gentle Death, when wilt thou come?
And take a Life that wearies me.

Tis not the Frost that freezes fell,
Nor blawing Snaw's Inclemency;
'Tis not sic Cauld that makes me cry,
But my Love's Heart grown cauld to me.

When we came in by *Glasgow Town*,
We were a comely Sight to see;
My love was cled in the black Velvet,
And I my sell in Cramasie.   *Crimson velvet*

But had I wist before I kiss'd,
That Love had been sae ill to win;
I'd lock'd my Heart in a Case of Gold,
And pinn'd it with a silver Pin.

Oh, oh! if my young Babe were born,
And set upon the Nurse's Knee,
And I my sell were dead and gane,
For a Maid again I'll never be.

Allan Ramsay was the first to publish this poignant lament of a forsaken girl in his Tea-Table Miscellany of c. 1724, and the almost identical version above is from Thomson's Orpheus Caledonius of 1733 (vol. I, no. 34). Traditionally the ballad refers to an unfortunate love affair at the court of Mary, Queen of Scots and perhaps even to Mary herself: Arthur's Seat and St Anthony's Well are close to Holyrood House, the Royal Palace in Edinburgh, and Mary's court

also visited Glasgow where Lord Darnley's father had a town house. Later versions of the ballad entitled 'Jamie Douglas' or 'The Marchioness of Douglas' refer to James, second Marquis of Douglas, and Lady Barbara Erskine who were married in 1670 and formally separated in 1681. William Lawrie, the marquis's chamberlain and possibly a disappointed lover, was blamed for stirring up trouble between the couple.

Moderate

Ye - streen the Queen had four Ma - ries, The night she'll hae but three;___ There's

Ma - ry Sea-ton an' Ma - ry Bea-ton, An' Ma - ry Car-mi-chael an' me.___

con Ped.

REPEAT FIRST VERSE AT THE END

Yestreen the Queen had four Maries,
The night she'll hae but three;
There's Mary Seaton an' Mary Beaton,
An' Mary Carmichael an' me.

Oh, often hae I dress'd my Queen,
An' put gowd in her hair,
But noo I've gotten for my reward
The gallows to be my share.

Oh, little did my mither ken,
The day she cradled me,
The land I was to travel in,
The death I was to dee.

Oh, happy, happy is the maid
That's born o' beauty free:
It was my dimplin rosy cheeks
That's been the dule o' me.   *grief*

There are many versions of this ballad. Some refer to infanticide, and are widely supposed to refer to an incident at the court of Mary, Queen of Scots, though there is no record of the song before the late 18th century. The Queen's Maries were her attendants – historically Mary Fleming, Mary Livingstone, Mary Seton and Mary Beaton – two of whose names appear in the final verse. No accusation of infanticide was ever made against any of the Queen's Maries, but a Frenchwoman and her lover, both in royal service, were hanged for murdering their child in 1563. In Russia one of Empress Catherine's maids of honour, a young woman called Mary Hamilton, was beheaded for infanticide in 1719 in the presence of the crown prince who probably fathered the child. The ballad possibly takes in both historical events. In Sharpe's Ballad Book *of 1823 the King, Henry Darnley, is implicated: Word's gane to the kitchen,/ And word's gane to the ha,/ That Marie Hamilton gangs wi bairn/ To the hichtest Stewart of a'.// She is sentenced to be hanged in Edinburgh for infanticide but meets her death with equanimity: 'Ye need nae weep for me,' she says,/ Ye need nae weep for me;/ For had I not slain my own sweet babe,/ This death I wadna dee.// 'Bring me a bottle of wine,' she says,/ ' The best that eer ye hae,/ That I may drink to my weil-wishers,/ And they may drink to me.'//*

Slow and tender

con Ped.

Ye banks and braes— o' bon - nie Doon,— How can— ye bloom— sae

fresh— and fair? How— can ye chant,—ye lit - tle birds,— And I— sae wea - ry

fu'— o' care! Thou'll break my heart,— thou warb - ling bird,— That

wan - tons through— the flow - er-ing— thorn: Thou— minds me o'— de-

par - ted joys,— De - par - ted ne - ver to— re - turn!

Ye banks and braes o' bonnie Doon,
How can ye bloom sae fresh and fair?
How can ye chant, ye little birds,
And I sae weary fu' o' care!
Thou'll break my heart, thou warbling bird,
That wantons through the flowering thorn:
Thou minds me o' departed joys,
Departed never to return!

Oft hae I rov'd by bonnie Doon,
To see the rose and woodbine twine;
And ilka bird sang o' its luve,
And fondly sae did I o' mine.
Wi' lightsome heart I pu'd a rose,
Fu' sweet upon its thorny tree;
And my fause luver staw my rose,   *lover stole*
But, ah! he left the thorn wi' me.

One of Burns's most famous songs, it was the revision of an earlier one ('Ye flowery banks o' bonnie Doon') and is included in the Scots Musical Museum *(vol. IV, no. 374). 'Do you know the history of the air?' he wrote to his publisher, George Thomson, in November 1794, 'it is curious enough. – a good many years ago, a Mr Jas Miller, Writer in your good town . . . expressed an ardent ambition to be able to compose a Scots air. – Mr Clarke, partly by way of joke, told him, to keep to the black keys of the harpsichord, and preserve some kind of rhythm; and he would infallibly compose a Scots air. – Certain it is, that in a few days, Mr Miller produced the rudiments of an air, which Mr Clarke, with some touches and corrections, fashioned into the tune in question.' It was first printed in Gow's* Second Collection of Strathspey Reels *(1788). Stephen Clarke was an Edinburgh organist who was Burns's musical advisor for the* Scots Musical Museum.

Tenderly, with feeling

con Ped.

Ae— fond kiss, and then— we se - ver! Ae— fare - weel, and then— for ev - er!

Deep— in heart wrung tears— I'll pledge thee, War - ring sighs and groans— I'll wage thee!

Who— shall say— that for - tune grieves him While— the star— of hope— she leaves— him?

Me,— nae cheer - fu' twin - kle lights— me; Dark— de - spair— a - round— be - nights me.

Ae fond kiss, and then we sever!
Ae fareweel, and then for ever!
Deep in heart-wrung tears I'll pledge thee,
Warring sighs and groans I'll wage thee!

Who shall say that fortune grieves him
While the star of hope she leaves him?
Me, nae chearfu' twinkle lights me;
Dark despair around benights me.

I'll ne'er blame my partial fancy,
Naething could resist my Nancy
But to see her, was to love her;
Love but her, and love for ever.

Had we never lov'd sae kindly,
Had we never lov'd sae blindly,
Never met – or never parted,
We had ne'er been broken-hearted.

Fare thee weel, thou first and fairest!
Fare thee weel, thou best and dearest!
Thine be ilka joy and treasure,   *every*
Peace, Enjoyment, Love, and Pleasure!

Ae fond kiss, and then we sever;
Ae fareweel, Alas! for ever!
Deep in heart-wrung tears I'll pledge thee,
Warring sighs and groans I'll wage thee!

This immortal love song was inspired by the poet's love for Mrs Nancy Maclehose or 'Clarinda' of the famous epistolary flirtation. Unusually for Burns, the relationship remained platonic and in December 1791 the lady, who was unhappily married, left Scotland to join her husband in the West Indies – hence the song. Of the fourth stanza, Sir Walter Scott wrote that these lines 'contain the essence of a thousand love tales', and exactly forty years later, Mrs Maclehose was to write in her journal: 'This day I can never forget. Parted with Burns, in the year 1791, never more to meet in this world. Oh, may we meet in heaven!' The tune, 'Rory Dall's Port', is printed in the Caledonian Pocket Companion *(1756): Rory Dall or Morrison (*Ruaidhri Mhic Mhuirich*) was born in Lewis around 1660 of a well-to-do tacksman, i.e. an agent who leased land from big landlords and sublet it to crofters. The son was destined for the Church until he contracted the smallpox which led to his blindness. He had a gift for music, so became a harper (a recognized profession for the blind in both Scotland and Ireland at the time) and was harper to the Macleods of Dunvegan for many years. Some of his poetry survives and various melodies bear his name.* Port *is simply a Gaelic word for tune. Two alternative settings have become popular in recent years, and the one below has all but supplanted 'Rory Dall's Port'.*

Ae fond kiss, and then we se-ver! Ae fare-weel, and then for ev-er!
Deep in heart-wrung tears I'll pledge thee, War-ring sighs and groans I'll wage thee!

Slowish

con Ped.

By— yon bon- nie banks and by yon bon- nie braes, Where the sun shines bright on Loch

Lo - mond, Where me and my true love were ev- er wont to gae, On the

bon- nie, bon- nie banks o' Loch Lo - mond. *O, ye'll   tak   the high road, An'*

I'll   tak the low road, And I'll   be in Scot-land a - fore   ye; But me and my true love will

ne - ver meet a - gain On the bon-nie, bon-nie banks o' Loch Lo - mond.

CHORUS AFTER EACH VERSE

By yon bonnie banks and by yon bonnie braes,
Where the sun shines bright on Loch Lomond,
Where me and my true love were ever wont to gae,
On the bonnie, bonnie banks o' Loch Lomond.

O, ye'll tak the high road, An' I'll tak the low road,
And I'll be in Scotland afore ye;
But me and my true love will never meet again
On the bonnie, bonnie banks o' Loch Lomond.

'Twas there that we parted in yon shady glen,
On the steep, steep side o' Ben Lomond,
Where in purple hue the Hieland hills we view,
And the moon coming out in the gloamin'.

The wee birdies sing and the wild flowers spring,
And in sunshine the waters are sleepin';
But the broken heart it kens, nae second spring again,
Tho' the waefu' may cease frae their greetin'!   *crying*

Traditionally these words are said to his sweetheart by a
Jacobite soldier about to be hung at Carlisle. The low road is
the grave by which his spirit will travel home almost at once.
Lady John Scott (1811–1900), folksong collector and com-
poser of 'Annie Laurie', got the tune from a poor boy singing
on the Edinburgh streets. Her own version opposite was not
published before 1850. A fragment found by Miss F. M.
Colquhoun of Luss says: We'll meet where we parted in bonnie
Luss Glen,/ Mang the heathery braes o' Ben Lomon',/ Starts
the roe frae the pass an' the fox frae his den,/ While abune
gleams the mune thro' the rowan.// Wi' yer bonnie laced shoon

an yer buckles sae clear,/ An' yer plaid ower yer shouther sae
rarely;/ Ae glance o' yer e'e wad chase awa' my fear,/ Sae
winsome are yer looks, O, my dearie!/

'Oh! whither away, my bonnie, bonnie May,
So late, an' so far in the gloamin'?
The mist gathers grey o'er muirland an' brae,
Oh! whither alane art thou roamin'?'

'I trysted my ain luve the nicht in the broom,
My Ranald, wha lo'es me sae dearly;
For the morrow he marches to Edinburgh toun,
To fecht for the King an' Prince Charlie!'

'Yet why weep ye sae, my bonnie, bonnie May,
Yer true luve from battle returnin',
His darlin' will claim in the micht o' his fame,
An' change into gladness her mournin!'

'Oh! weel may I weep – yestreen in my sleep
We stood bride an' bridegroom thegither!
But his lips an' his breath were as chilly as death,
An' his heart's bluid was red on the heather!

'Oh! dauntless in battle as tender in love,
He'll yield ne'er a foot to the foeman;
But never again frae the field o' the slain
To Moira he'll come an' Loch Lomon'.

'Oh! he'll gang the hie road an' I'll gang the low,
But I'll be in Heaven afore him;
For my bed is prepar'd in the mossy graveyard,
Mang the hazels o' green Inverarnan.'

Lively

My— love, she's but a lass-ie yet, My— love, she's but a lass-ie yet; We'll—

con Ped.

let her stand a year or twa, She'll no— be— half sae sau-cy yet; I—

rue the day I sought her, O! I— rue the day I sought her, O! Wha—

gets her needs na say he's woo'd, But he— may— say he's bought her, O!

My love, she's but a lassie yet,
My love, she's but a lassie yet;
We'll let her stand a year or twa,
She'll no be half sae saucy yet;

I rue the day I sought her, O!
I rue the day I sought her, O!
Wha gets her needs na say he's woo'd,
But he may say he's bought her, O!

Come draw a drap o' the best o't yet,
Come draw a drap o' the best o't yet:
Gae seek for pleasure whare ye will,
But here I never misst it yet.

We're a' dry wi' drinking o't,
We're a' dry wi' drinking o't:
The minister kisst the fiddler's wife,
He couldna preach for thinkin o't.

Throughout his life Burns was greatly preoccupied by the conflict between love and money – see 'She's fair and fause' and 'My tocher's the jewel'. 'My love she's but a lassie yet' is sung by a man who has ventured into the world of husband-seekers, only to be rejected on account of his poverty. He retires, bruised and humiliated, to the masculine world of the tavern with its more dependable pleasures. The catchy perpetuum mobile *tune appeared in Bremner's* Reels *as 'Miss Farquharson's Reel' and with Burns's words in the* Scots Musical Museum *of 1790 (vol. III, no. 225). In this, as in many other songs, Burns was inspired by an existing folksong. The last four lines appear in the 1776 edition of Herd's* Scottish Songs *(as 'Green grow the rashes O') and the first two are traditional. James Hogg's version was popular in the 19th century.*

My love she's but a lassie yet,
A lightsome lovely lassie yet;
It scarce would do
To sit an' woo
Down by the stream sae glassy yet,
But there's a braw time comin' yet,
When we may gang a-roamin' yet,
An' hint wi' glee
O' joys to be,
When fa's the modest gloamin' yet.

She's nither proud nor saucy yet,
She's neither plump nor gaucy yet;   *portly*
But just a jinkin';
Bonnie Blinkin'
Hilty-skilty lassie yet.
But O her artless smile's mair sweet
Than hinny or than marmalete;
An' right or wrang,
Ere it be lang,
I'll bring her to a parley yet.

I'm jealous o' what blesses her,
The very breeze that kisses her,
The flowery beds on which she treads,
Though wae for ane that misses her.
Then O to meet my lassie yet,
Up in yon glen sae grassy yet;
For all I see
Are nought to me
Save her that's but a lassie yet!

CHORUS AFTER EACH VERSE

I am my mammy's ae bairn,   *only child*
Wi' unco folk I weary, Sir,   *strange*
And lying in a man's bed,
I'm fley'd it mak me eerie, Sir.   *frightened/ gloomy*

I'm o'er young, I'm o'er young,
I'm o'er young to marry yet!
I'm o'er young, twad be a sin
To tak me frae my mammy yet.

Hallowmass is come and gane,   *All Saints*
The nights are lang in winter, Sir;
And you an' I in ae bed,
In trowth, I dare na venture, Sir.

Fu' loud and shrill the frosty wind
Blaws thro' the leafless timmer, Sir;   *wood*
But if ye come this gate again,   *way*
I'll aulder be gin simmer, Sir.   *by summer*

Burns wrote of 'I'm o'er young to marry yet': 'the chorus of this song
is very old; the rest of it, such as it is, is mine'. The poet's modesty is
characteristic. The song is actually a subtle portrayal of a young girl
before puberty, shy and blushing, but with a real awareness of her
sexual future. In the last verse her reluctance gives way to a flirtatious
readiness. The tune appears in various 18th-century collections, and
with Burns's words in the Scots Musical Museum *(vol. II, no. 107).*
The song has remained popular ever since though the original tune
has been almost entirely displaced by this lively strathspey below: —

She's fair and fause that caus-es my smart; I lo'ed her mei-kle and lang; She's bro-ken her vow, she's bro-ken my heart, And I may e'en gae hang. A coof cam' in wi' routh o' gear, And I hae tint my dear-est dear; But wo-man is but warld's gear, Sae let the bon-nie lass gang!

She's fair and fause that causes my smart;   *false*
I lo'ed her meikle and lang;   *much and long*
She's broken her vow, she's broken my heart,
And I may e'en gae hang.
A coof cam' in wi' routh o' gear,   *fool with much money*
And I hae tint my dearest dear;   *have lost*
But woman is but warld's gear,   *wordly goods*
Sae let the bonnie lass gang!

Whae'er ye be that woman love,
To this be never blind,
Nae ferlie 'tis tho' fickle she prove,   *no wonder*
A woman has't by kind:
A woman, lovely woman fair!
An angel form's faun to thy share,   *fallen*
'Twad been o'er meikle to gien thee mair,   *too much*
I mean an angel mind.

This song was published in 1792 in Johnson's Scots Musical Museum *(vol. IV, no. 398) but it was probably written some years before. Burns's lawyer friend Alexander Cunningham had been engaged to marry Anne Stewart (the subject of 'Anna, thy charms my bosom fire') but she jilted him in favour of a richer suitor, Forrest Dewar, who was a surgeon in Edinburgh. Burns was prompted to write an indignant letter of condolence (and this song) to his friend on reading an account of Anne's marriage and he returned to the theme with 'Had I a cave on some wild distant shore' to the tune 'Robin Adair'. Love and money, and their conflicting interests, preoccupied the poet throughout his life – as in 'My tocher's the jewel'. The tune is from the* Caledonian Pocket Companion *of 1752.*

Moderate

O, mei - kle thinks my luve o'___ my beau - ty, And mei - kle thinks my___ luve

o'___ my kin; But lit - tle thinks my luve I___ ken braw - lie My

toch - er's the je - wel has charms for him. It's a' for the ap - ple he'll

nou - rish the tree; It's a' for the hin - ny he'll che - rish the bee; My

con Ped.

lad-die's sae mei-kle in love wi' the sil-ler, He can-na hae luve— to spare— for me!

O, meikle thinks my luve o' my beauty,   *a lot*
And meikle thinks my luve o' my kin;
But little thinks my luve I ken brawlie   *know well*
My tocher's the jewel has charms for him.   *dowry*
It's a' for the apple he'll nourish the tree;
It's a' for the hinny he'll cherish the bee;
My laddie's sae meikle in love wi' the siller,   *money*
He canna hae luve to spare for me!

Your proffer o' luve's an airle-penny,   *earnest money*
My tocher's the bargain ye wad buy;
But an ye be crafty, I am cunnin,
Sae ye wi' anither your fortune maun try.   *must*
Ye're like to the timmer o' yon rotten wood,   *timber*
Ye're like to the bark o' yon rotten tree,
Ye'll slip frae me like a knotless thread,
And ye'll crack your credit wi' mae nor me.   *more than*

Burns sent the last four lines of this song to Tytler of Woodhouselee in August 1787 'as a sample of the old pieces that are still to be found among our Peasantry in the West. I once had a great many of these fragments and some of these here entire; but as I had no idea then that anybody cared for them, I have forgot them.' Nathaniel Gow included the tune, entitled 'Lord Elcho's favourite', in one of his Collections, but Burns knew it from earlier sources as 'The highway to Edinburgh'. 'This song is to be sung to the air called Lord Elcho's favourite,' he remarked, 'but do not put that name above it, let it just pass for the tune of the song, and a beautiful tune it is.' (To 'crack your credit' is to become bankrupt or lose your reputation.)

WEDDINGS
LULLABIES
MARRIAGE

Moderate

The Laird o' Cock - pen, he's proud and he's great, His mind is taen up wi' the things o' the State; He wan - ted a wife his braw house to keep, But fa - vour wi' woo - in' was fash - ious to seek.

con Ped.

The Laird o' Cockpen, he's proud and he's great,
His mind is taen up wi' the things o' the State;
He wanted a wife his braw house to keep,
But favour wi' wooin' was fashious to seek.   *troublesome*

Doon by the dyke-side a lady did dwell:
At his table head he thocht she'd look well –
M'Clish's ae dochter o' Claverse-ha'-Lee,
A penniless lass wi' a lang pedigree.

His wig was weel pouthered, – as guid as when new,
His waistcoat was white and his coat it was blue;
He put on a ring, a sword, and cock'd hat –
And wha could refuse the Laird wi' a' that?

He took his grey mare and he rade cannily,   *gently*
And he rapp'd at the yett o' Claverse-ha'-Lee: –   *gate*
'Gae, tell Mistress Jean to come speedily ben;
She's wanted to speak to the Laird o' Cockpen.'

Mistress Jean she was makin' the elder-flower wine: –
'And what brings the Laird at sic a like time?'
She put aff her apron an' on her silk goon,
Her mutch wi' red ribbons and gaed awa' doon.

And when she came ben he bowed fu' low,
And what was his errand he soon let her know;
Amazed was the Laird, when the leddy said 'Na!'
As wi' a laigh curtsie she turned awa'!   *low*

Dumbfoundered was he, but nae sigh did he gie,
He mounted his mare and he rade cannilie;
And aften he thocht as he ga'ed through the glen, –
'She's daft to refuse the Laird o' Cockpen!'

*The result of the laird's proposal puts him among the rejected lovers,
but he scrapes into this section through these two verses of inferior
merit added by a Miss Ferrier, though they are sometimes attributed
to Sir Alexander Bothwell: But noo that the Laird his exit had made,/
Mistress Jean, she reflected on what she had said;/ 'For ane I'll get
better, its waur I'll get ten –/ I was daft to refuse the Laird o' Cockpen.'/
/ Neist time that the Laird and the leddy were seen,/ They were gaun
arm in arm to the Kirk on the green;/ Noo she sits in the ha' like a
weel tappit hen,/ But as yet there's nae chickens appear'd at Cockpen!///(A
tappit hen is one which is tufted or crested. Lids shaped like them were
used to cover plates of new-laid eggs, since the crest could be used as
a lifting knob.) Herd published a version of 'The Laird of Cockpen'
in 1776: And was nae Cockpen right saucy?/ And was nae Cockpen
right saucy?/ He len'd his lady to gentlemen/ And kist the collier
lassie.// The estate of Cockpen was situated south of Edinburgh
(handy for the Lothian coal-mines) and several Cockpen street names
survive in the district to this day. Claverseha' Lea is said to have been
Catcane Castle, now a ruin within the grounds of Harvieston House,
near Gorebridge. Burns contributed 'When she cam ben she bobbed'
to Johnson's Scots Musical Museum of 1792 (vol. IV, no. 353) and the
now much more widely-known 'Laird o' Cockpen' was written by
Lady Nairne (1766–1845) a pious but kindly Perthshire aristocrat
who was inspired to prune and refine the verses of the song-loving
Scottish peasantry, ridding the old songs of their indelicate, not to
mention gross, sentiments. Like her contemporary Robert Burns,
she took old tunes and put new words to them, fit for consumption
in the most genteel Edinburgh drawing rooms, where they were
sung preferably without the addition of 'artificial' instrumental
accompaniments.*

O when she cam ben she bobbed fu' law,
O when she cam ben she bobbed fu' law,
And when she cam ben she kiss'd Cockpen,
And syne deny'd she did it at a'.

And was na Cockpen right saucy witha',
And was na Cockpen right saucy witha',
In leaving the dochter of a lord,
And kissin a Collier lassie and a',

O never look down, my lassie at a',
O never look down, my lassie at a',
Thy lips are as sweet and thy figure compleat,
As the finest dame in castle or ha',

Tho' has nae silk and holland sae sma,
Tho' has nae silk and holland sae sma,
Thy coat and thy sark are thy ain handywark
And Lady Jean was never sae braw.

Very lively

In June, when broom in bloom was seen, And brack-en waved fu' fresh and green, And

warm the sun, wi' sil - ver sheen, The hills and glens did glad-den, O; Ae

day, up - on the Bor - der bent, The tink - lers pitch'd their gyp - sy tent, And

auld and young, wi' ae con-sent, Re - solved to haud a wad-din', O. *Dir-rim day doo a day,*

Dir-rim doo   a da dee, O,   Dir-rim day   doo   a day, Hur-rah for the tink-lers' wad-din', O.

In June, when broom in bloom was seen,
And bracken waved fu' fresh and green,
And warm the sun, wi' silver sheen,
The hills and glens did gladden, O;
Ae day, upon the Border bent,
The tinklers pitch'd their gypsy tent,
And auld and young, wi' ae consent,
Resolved to haud a waddin', O.

Dirrim day doo a day,
Dirrim doo a da dee, O,
Dirrim day doo a day,
Hurrah for the tinklers' waddin', O.

The bridegroom was wild Norman Scott,
Wha thrice had broke the nuptial knot,
And ance was sentenced to be shot
For breach o' martial orders, O.
His gleesome joe was Madge MaKell,   *fortuneteller*
A spaewife, match for Nick himsel',
Wi' glamour, cantrip, charm, and spell,   *witchcraft, magic*
She frichted baith the Borders, O.   *frightened*

Dirrim day doo a day,
Dirrim doo a da dee, O,
Dirrim day doo a day,
Hurrah for the tinklers' waddin', O.

Nae priest was there, wi' solemn face,
Nae clerk to claim o' crowns a brace;
The piper and fiddler played the grace
To set their gabs a-steerin', O.   *mouths working*
Mang beef and mutton, pork and veal,
Mang paunches, plucks, and fresh cow-heel,
Fat haggises, and cauler jeel,   *cold jelly*
They clawed awa' careerin', O.

Dirrim day doo a day,
Dirrim doo a da dee, O,
Dirrim day doo a day,
Hurrah for the tinklers' waddin', O.

Fresh salmon, newly taen in Tweed,
Saut ling and cod o' Shetland breed,
They worried, till kytes were like to screed,   *bellies rip*
Mang flagons and flasks o' gravy, O.
There was raisin-kail and sweet-milk saps,   *broth*
And ewe-milk cheese in whangs and flaps,   *chunks & slices*
And they rookit, to gust their gabs and craps,*
Richt mony a cadger's cavie, O.   *grumbler's hen-coop*
                                stole to stuff their mouths and bellies

Dirrim day doo a day,
Dirrim doo a da dee, O,
Dirrim day doo a day,
Hurrah for the tinklers' waddin', O.

The drink flew round in wild galore,
And soon upraised a hideous roar
Blithe Comus ne'er a queerer core
Saw seated round his table, O.
They drank, they danced, they swore, they sang,
They quarrell'd and greed the hale day lang,
And the wranglin' that rang amang the thrang
Wad match'd the tongues o' Babel, O.

Dirrim day doo a day,
Dirrim doo a da dee, O,
Dirrim day doo a day,
Hurrah for the tinklers' waddin', O.

The drink gaed dune before their drooth,
That vexed baith mony a maw and mooth,
It damp'd the fire o' age and youth,
And every breast did sadden, O;
Till three stout loons flew ower the fell,
At risk o' life, their drouth to quell,
And robb'd a neebourin' smuggler's stell,   *(whisky) still*
To carry on the waddin', O.

Dirrim day doo a day,
Dirrim doo a da dee, O,
Dirrim day doo a day,
Hurrah for the tinklers' waddin', O.

Wi' thunderin' shouts they hail'd them back,
To broach the barrels they werena slack,
While the fiddler's plane-tree leg they brak'
For playin' 'Farewell to Whisky, O'.
Delirium seized the roarous thrang,
The bagpipes in the fire they flang,
And sowtherin' airns on riggin's rang,   *soldering irons*
The drink play'd siccan a plisky, O.   *such a trick*

Dirrim day doo a day,
Dirrim doo a da dee, O,
Dirrim day doo a day,
Hurrah for the tinklers' waddin', O.

The sun fell laich owre Solway banks,   *low*
While on they plied their roughsome pranks,
And the stalwart shadows o' their shanks,
Wide ower the muir were spreadin', O.
Till, heads and thraws, amang the whins,
They fell wi' broken brows and shins,
And sair craist banes filled mony skins,
To close the tinklers' waddin', O.

Dirrim day doo a day,
Dirrim doo a da dee, O,
Dirrim day doo a day,
Hurrah for the tinklers' waddin', O.

The Oxford English Dictionary *defines tinkers or tinklers as craftsmen, usually itinerant, who mend pots, kettles and other household utensils. The term applies, less flatteringly, to travelling beggars, traders and performers, as well as vagabonds, tramps, and reputed thieves. In Scotland they are often descended from those evicted from their lands by enemy clans, and have only vagrancy in common with gypsies, a race of Hindi origin which first entered Europe in the 14th century.*

Before 1940 marriage was not a sacred ceremony in Scots law and could be legally performed by anyone, which is why the blacksmith of Gretna Green used to marry couples eloping from England. Being free to invent their own marriage ceremonies some Scots swore an oath on a bible held over a running stream – Burns is supposed to have married Highland Mary in that way. Flinging their soldering irons over a rooftree (the 'riggins') seems to have been favoured by tinkers. This song was written by William Watt (1792–1859), who was born in West Linton in Peeblesshire. As well as being a weaver, Watt painted, wrote poetry and music ('Kate Dalrymple' is his best-known song) and was a Parish Church precentor. 'The Tinklers' Waddin'' used to be very popular in rural Scotland but has more recently been overtaken by its Glasgow-born parody, 'Rothesay, O'.

One Hogmanay at Glesca Fair,
There was me, mysel' and sev'ral mair,
We a' went off to hae a tear   *part)*
An spend the nicht in Rothesay, O.
We wandered thro' the Broomielaw,
Thro' wind an' rain an' sleet an' snaw,
And at forty minutes after twa,
We got the length o' Rothesay, O.

A dirrum a doo a dum a day,
A dirrum a doo a daddy O
A dirrum a doo a dum a day,
The day we went to Rothesay, O.

A sodger lad named Ru'glen Will,
Wha's regiment's lyin, at Barra Hill,
Gaed off wi' a tanner to get a gill
In a public hoose in Rothesay, O.
Said he 'I think I'd like to sing'
Said I 'Ye'll no dae sic a thing'
He said Clear the room and I'll mak' a ring
And I'll fecht them all in Rothesay, O.

A dirrum a doo a dum a day,
A dirrum a doo a daddy O
A dirrum a doo a dum a day,
The day we went to Rothesay, O.

In search of lodgins we did slide,
To find a place where we could bide;
There was eighty-twa o' us inside
In a single room in Rothesay, O.
We a' lay doon to tak' our ease,
When somebody happened for to sneeze,
And he wakened half a million fleas
In a single room in Rothesay, O.

A dirrum a doo a dum a day,
A dirrum a doo a daddy O
A dirrum a doo a dum a day,
The day we went to Rothesay, O.

There were several different kinds of bugs,
Some had feet like dyer's clogs,
And they sat on the bed and they cockit their lugs,
And cried 'Hurrah for Rothesay, O!
'A noo,' says I, we'll have to 'lope'
So we went and joined the Band O'Hope,
But the polis wouldna let us stop
Another nicht in Rothesay, O.

A dirrum a doo a dum a day,
A dirrum a doo a daddy O
A dirrum a doo a dum a day,
The day we went to Rothesay, O.

Rothesay is a holiday resort on the Isle of Bute in the Firth of
Clyde. In the first half of the 20th century, when excursions
'doon the watter' were the favourite outings of the Glasgow
working classes, the town was the final destination for the
steam paddle boats sailing from the Broomielaw quay in
Glasgow. The trips were especially popular during the 'Glesca
Fair': a two-week holiday in late July, when even the furnaces
of the ironworks were extinguished and the smoke covering the
Clyde valley was allowed to clear. The only other regular
festival in the working Glaswegians' calendar was Hogmanay,
the traditional Scottish New Year celebration, which explains
why the singer confuses them in the song's first line. The Band
of Hope was a self-improvement society mainly run by clergy-
men, women and reformed alcoholics, whose members swore
to abstain from strong drink.

Moderate

Will ye gang to the— Hie - lands, Lee - zie Lind - say? Will ye

con Ped.

gang to the— Hie - lands wi'— me? Will ye gang to the—

Hie - lands, Leez - ie Lind - say, My pride— and my dar - ling to— be?

Will ye gang to the Hielands, Leezie Lindsay?
Will ye gang to the Hielands wi' me?
Will ye gang to the Hielands, Leezie Lindsay,
My pride and my darling to be?

To gang to the Hielands wi' you, Sir,
I dinna ken how that may be,
For I ken nae the road I am gaeing,
Nor yet wha I'm gaun wi'.

'Oh, Leezie, lass, ye maun ken little,
Syn ye dinna ken me,
For I am Lord Ronald Mac Donald,
A chieftain o' high degree.'

'Oh, if ye're the laird o' Mac Donald,
A great ane I ken ye maun be;
But how can a chieftain sae mighty
Think o' a puir lassie like me.'

She has gotten a gown o' green satin,
She has kilted it up to her knee,
And she's aff wi' Lord Ronald Mac Donald,
His bride and his darling to be.

Burns contributed just a fragment of this ballad to the Scots Musical Museum *of 1796 (no. 434): 'Will ye go to the Highlands, Leezie Lindsay?/ Will ye go to the Highlands wi' me? / Will ye go to the Highlands, Leezie Lindsay, / My pride and my darling to be?'). He clearly intended to extend this, as Johnson, editor of the* Museum *wrote on the poet's MS: 'Mr Burns is to send words.' Smith's* Scotish Minstrel *of 1820–24 added an additional four stanzas, and a complete version of the ballad was published in Jamieson's* Popular Ballads *in 1806. There are many variants of this story of young Donald MacDonald, heir of Kingcausie, who goes to Edinburgh to find a bride, under strict instructions from his mother to present himself as a poor man and to offer to 'the bonny ladies' only curds and whey, and a bed of bracken. A Mearns tradition identifies the lady as a daughter of Lindsay of Edzell.*

Step we gai-ly, on we go,   Heel for heel and toe for toe,   Arm in arm and row in row,

All for Mai-ri's wed-ding.   O-ver hill-ways up and down,   Myr-tle green and brack-en brown,

Past the shiel-ings, thro' the town; All for sake of Mai-ri.   Step we gai-ly, on we go,

Heel for heel and toe for toe,   Arm in arm and row in row,   All for Mai-ri's wed-ding.

CHORUS AFTER EACH VERSE

Step we gaily, on we go,
Heel for heel and toe for toe,
Arm in arm and row in row,
All for Mairi's wedding.

Over hillways up and down,
Myrtle green and bracken brown,
Past the shielings, thro' the town;
All for sake of Mairi.

Step we gaily, on we go,
Heel for heel and toe for toe,
Arm in arm and row in row,
All for Mairi's wedding.

Red her cheeks as rowans are,
Bright her eyes as any star,
Fairest o' them a' by far
Is our darling Mairi.

Step we gaily, on we go,
Heel for heel and toe for toe,
Arm in arm and row in row,
All for Mairi's wedding.

Plenty herring, plenty meal,
Plenty peat to fill her creel,
Plenty bonny bairns as weel;
That's the toast for Mairi.

Step we gaily, on we go,
Heel for heel and toe for toe,
Arm in arm and row in row,
All for Mairi's wedding.

This catchy traditional tune was published in the nineteenth century by Dr Peter MacLeod (1797–1859) who edited a four-volume collection of Scottish songs. It was popularized by Sir Hugh Roberton (conductor of Glasgow's famous Orpheus Choir) who wrote these English words and arranged it for his Songs of the Isles, *published in 1950.*

Fairly slow

O, can ye sew Cu - shions and can ye sew Sheets? And can ye— sing—

bal - lu - loo— when the bairn greets? And hee and baw bir - die and

hee and baw lamb; And hee and baw bir - die, my bon - nie wee lamb.

Lively

Hee O, wee O, what wou'd I do wi' you? Black's the life that I lead wi' you

Slow

Mon-ny o' you lit-tle for to gie you Hee O, wee O, what wou'd I do wi' you?

O, can ye sew Cushions and can ye sew Sheets?
And can ye sing balluloo when the bairn greets?   *weeps*
And hee and baw birdie and hee and baw lamb;
And hee and baw birdie, my bonnie wee lamb.

Hee O, wee O, what wou'd I do wi' you?
Black's the life that I lead wi' you
Monny o' you little for to gie you
Hee O, wee O, what wou'd I do wi' you?

I biggit the cradle upon the treetop,   *built*
And aye as the wind blew, my cradle did rock.
And hush a baw baby, O ba lil li loo.
And hee and baw birdie, my bonnie wee doo.

Now hush a baw lammie, and hush a baw dear,
Does wee lammie ken that its daddie's no here?   *know*
The wild wind is ravin', thy minnie's heart sair,
The wild wind is ravin', but ye dinna care.

Sing bal la loo lammie, sing bal la loo dear,
Does wee lammie ken that its daddie's no here?
Ye're rockin' fu' sweetly on mammie's warm knee,
But daddie's a rockin' upon the saut sea.

This lovely old lullaby with its interesting change of rhythm in the second part (perfect for its purpose) appeared in Johnson's Scots Musical Museum *of 1796 (vol. V, no. 444). The last three stanzas are later additions, and if used, treat 'Hee O, wee O' as a chorus.*

Fairly slow

Cag - ar-an, cag - ar-an, cag - ar-an gaol-ach, Cag - ar-an fogh-ain-teach, fear de mo dhaoin-e,

con *Ped.*

Goi - didh e go - bhar dhomh, goi - didh e caoir - ich;

Goi - didh e cap - ull is mart o na raoin - tean.

Cagaran, cagaran, cagaran gaolach,
Cagaran foghainteach, fear de mo dhaoine,
Goididh e gobhar dhomh, goididh e caoirich;
Goididh e capull us mart o na raointean.

Cagaran laghach thu, cagaran caomh thu,
Cagaran odhar, na cluinneam do chaoine;
Goididh e gobhar us goididh e caorich,
Goididh e sithionn o fhireach an aonaich.

Dean an cadalan 's duin do shùilean;
Dean an cadalan beag ann mo sgùrdaich;
Rinn thu an cadalan, 's dhùin do shùilean;
Rinn thu an cadalan, slàn gu'n dùisg thu.

Hush ye, my bairnie, my bonnie wee lammie;
Routh o' guid things ye shall bring tae yer mammie;   *plenty*
Hare frae the meadow, and deer frae the mountain
Grouse frae the muirlan', and trout frae the fountain.

Hush ye, my bairnie, my bonnie wee dearie;
Sleep! come and close the een, heavy and wearie;
Closed are the wearie een, rest are ye takin' –
Soun' be yer sleepin', and bright be yer wakin'.

This gentle lullaby was translated from the Gaelic by Malcolm Macfarlane (who translated 'The Mist-Covered Mountains of Home' also). He was editor of Songs of the Highlands.

CHORUS AFTER EACH VERSE

Dh'fhàg mi'n so 'na shìneadh e,
'Na shìneadh e, 'na shìneadh e;
Gu'n d'fhàg mi'n so 'na shìneadh e
Nuair d'fhalbh mi bhuain nam braoileagan.

Hòbhan, hòbhan, Goiridh òg O,
Goiridh òg O, goiridh òg O;
Hòbhan, hòbhan, Goiridh òg O,
Gu'n d'fhalbh mo ghaol s gu'n d'fhàg e mi.

Fhuair mi lorg an dòbhrain duinn,
An dòbhrain duinn, an dòbhrain duinn;
Gu'n d'fhuair mi lorg an dòbhrain duinn;
'S cha d'fhuair mi lorg mo chòineachain!

Fhuair mi lorg na h-eal' air an t-snàmh,
Na h-eal' air an t-snàmh, na h-eal' air an t-snàmh,
Gu'n d'fhuair mi lorg na h-eal' air an t-snàmh,
'S cha d'fhuair mi lorg mo chòineachain!

Fhuair mi lorg an laoigh bhric dheirg,
An laoigh bhric dheirg, an laoigh bhric dheirg,
Gu'n d'fhuair mi lorg an laoigh bhric dheirg,
'S cha d'fhuair mi lorg mo chòineachain!

Fhuair mi lorg a' cheò sa bheinn,
A' cheò sa bheinn, a' cheò sa bheinn;
Ged fhuair mi lorg a' cheò sa bheinn,
Cha d'fhuair mi lorg mo chòineachain!

This song of a mother whose child was stolen by fairies was translated by Lachlan Macbean who is also responsible for the equally popular 'Child in the manger'. The theme is a common one in Scottish folklore: often the mother would find a weakly changeling left by the fairies in exchange for her strong, healthy baby.

I left my darling lying here,
A-lying here, a-lying here,
I left my darling lying here,
To go and gather blaeberries.

Hovan, hovan, Gorry og O,
Gorry og O, Gorry og O;
Hovan, hovan, Gorry og O,
I've lost my darling baby O!

I've found the wee brown otter's track,
The otter's track, the otter's track,
I've found the wee brown otter's track,
But ne'er a trace of baby, O!

I found the track of the swan on the lake,
The swan on the lake, the swan on the lake;
I found the track of the swan on the lake,
But not the track of baby, O!

I found the track of the yellow fawn,
The yellow fawn, the yellow fawn,
I found the track of the yellow fawn,
But could not trace my baby, O!

I found the trail of the mountain mist,
The mountain mist, the mountain mist,
I found the trail of the mountain mist,
But ne'er a trace of baby, O!

Moderate

Al - ly, bal - ly, al - ly, bal - ly bee, Sit - tin' on yer mam - my's knee,

con Ped.

Gree - tin' for a - nith - er baw - bee, Tae buy mair Coul - ter's Can - dy.

Ally, bally, ally, bally bee,
Sittin' on yer mammy's knee,
Greetin' for anither baw-bee,   *another sixpence*
Tae buy mair Coulter's Candy.

Ally, bally, ally, bally bee,
When you grow up you'll go to sea,
Makin pennies for your daddy and me,
Tae buy mair Coulter's Candy.

Mammy gie me ma thrifty doon   *my money-box*
Here's auld Coulter comin' roon
Wi' a basket on his croon   *crown*
Selling Coulter's Candy.

Little Annie's greetin' tae
Sae whit can puir wee Mammy dae
But gie them a penny atween them twae
Tae buy mair Coulter's Candy.

Poor wee Jeanie's lookin' affa thin,   *awfully*
A rickle o' banes covered ower wi' skin,   *bag of bones*
Noo she's gettin' a double chin
Wi' sookin' Coulter's Candy.

Robert Coltart was a confectioner who made and sold his
own sweets in the Borders around the turn of the century.
He was a colourful figure with a 'big lum hat' at local
markets and fairs, and the first verse of this song was his
advertising jingle – not that the Scots ever needed much
persuasion to indulge in sweeties! Norman Buchan added
the third verse, and this version is the one sung by Roddy
McMillan, Scots actor, playwright and folk-singer.

LEANABH AN AIGH *MARY MACDONALD*

With a lilt

Lean- abh an àigh, an lean- abh aig Màir - i, Rug- adh san stàb - all, Rìgh nan Dùl; Thàin-ig don fhàs - ach, dh'fhuil-ing'nar n-àit - e Son' iad an àir - eamh bhith- eas dha dlùth!

con Ped.

Leanabh an àigh, an leanabh aig Màiri,
Rugadh san stàball, Rìgh nan Dùl;
Thàinig don fhàsach, dh'fhuiling 'nar n-àite
Son' iad an àireamh bhitheas dha dlùth!

Ged a bhios leanabain aig rìghrean na talmhainn
An greadhnachas garbh is anabarr mùirn,
'S geàrr gus am falbh iad, 's fàsaidh iad anfhann,
An àilleachd 's an dealbh a' searg san ùir.

Cha b'ionann 's an t-Uan thàinig gar fuasgladh –
Iriosal, stuama ghluais e'n tùs;
E naomh gun truailleachd, Cruithfhear an t-sluaigh,
Dh'èirich e suas le buaidh on ùir.

Leanabh an àigh, mar dh'aithris na fàidhean;
'S na h-àinglean àrd', b'e miann an sùl;
'S E 's airidh air gràdh 's air urram thoirt dhà –
Sona an àireamh bhitheas dhà dlùth.

The original of this popular childrens' carol (which is in the
current Church Hymnary) *was written by Mary Macdonald*
(1817–c.1890) of the island of Mull, and the old Gaelic
melody to which it was set in 1917 was named 'Bunessan' after
her birthplace. Lachlan Macbean (1853–1931) from Kiltarlity
was editor of Scottish Songs and Hymns of the Gael *(1888)*
and as well as writing and translating songs such as 'A Fairy
Lullaby' he compiled The Celtic Who's Who. *The hymn*
'Morning has broken' was written by Eleanor Farjeon (1881–
1965) to the tune 'Bunessan' and like Newton's 'Amazing
grace' it achieved considerable fame as a pop song in the 70s.

Child in the manger, Infant of Mary;
Outcast and stranger, Lord of all!
Child who inherits all our transgressions,
All our demerits on Him fall.

Once the most holy Child of salvation
Gently and lowly lived below;
Now, as our glorious Mighty Redeemer,
See Him victorious o'er each foe.

Prophets foretold Him, Infant of wonder;
Angels behold Him on his throne;
Worthy our Saviour of all their praises;
Happy for ever are His own.

JOHN GRUMLIE

Lively

con Ped.

John Grum - lie swore by the licht o' the moon And the green leaves on the

tree_____ That he could do more work in a day Than his wife could do____ in

three._____ His__ wife rose up in the mor - ning, Wi cares an' trou - bles e -

now;_____ 'John Grum - lie bide at hame, John, and I'll gae haud the

plow.' *Sing - ing fal de lal lal de ral lal, Fa lal lal lal lal la!___* 'John

Grum - lie bide at hame, John, And I'll gae haud___ the plow.'___

John Grumlie swore by the licht o' the moon
And the green leaves on the tree
That he could do more work in a day
Than his wife could do in three.
His wife rose up in the morning,
Wi cares an' troubles enow; –
'John Grumlie bide at hame, John, and
I'll gae haud the plow.'
Singing fal de lal lal de ral lal,
Fa lal lal lal lal la!
'John Grumlie bide at hame, John,
And I'll gae haud the plow.'

'First ye maun dress your children fair,
And put them in a' their gear,
And ye maun turn the malt, John,
Or else ye'll spoil the beer.
And ye maun reel the tweel, John,   *wind the twill*
That I span yesterday;
And ye maun ca' in the hens, John,
Else they'll a' lay away.'
Singing fal de lal lal de ral lal,
Fa lal lal lal lal la!
'And ye maun ca' in the hens, John,
Else they'll a' lay away.'

O, he did dress his children fair,
And he put them in a' their gear,
But he forgot to turn the malt,
And so he spoiled the beer.
And he sang aloud as he reel'd the tweel
That his wife span yesterday;
But he forgot to put up the hens,
And the hens a' lay'd away.
Singing fal de lal lal de ral lal,
Fa lal lal lal lal la!
But he forgot to put up the hens,
And the hens a' lay'd away.

The hawkit crummie loot down nae milk;   *spotted cow*
He kirned, nor butter gat;   *churned*
And a' gaed wrang, and nought gaed richt,   *went wrong*
He danced wi' rage, and grat.   *cried*
Then up he ran to the head o' the knowe,
Wi' mony a wave an' shout,
She heard him as she heard him not,
And steered the stots about.   *guided the bullocks*
Singing fal de lal lal de ral lal,
Fa lal lal lal lal la!
She heard him as she heard him not,
And steered the stots about.

John Grumlie's wife cam' hame at e'en,
And laughed as she'd been mad,
When she saw the house in siccan a plicht,   *such a*
And John sae glum and sad.
Quoth he, 'I gie up my housewifeskep, *housewife's cap*
I'll be nae mair gudewife;'
'Indeed,' quo she, 'I'm weel content,
Ye may keep it the rest o' your life.'
Singing fal de lal lal de ral lal,
Fa lal lal lal lal la!
'Indeed,' quo she, 'I'm weel content,
Ye may keep it the rest o' your life.'

'The deil be in that,' quo surly John,
'I'll do as I've done before,'
Wi' that the gudewife took up a stoot rung,
And John made aff to the door.
'Stop, stop, gudewife, I'll haud my tongue,
I ken I'm sair to blame;
But henceforth I maun mind the plow,
And ye maun bide at hame.'
Singing fal de lal lal de ral lal,
Fa lal lal lal lal la!
'But henceforth I maun mind the plow,
And ye maun bide at hame.'

'John Grumlie' itself was considered 'ancient' in 19th-century song-books but its sentiments (most women would agree) are as relevant today. 'John Grumlie' is apparently based on the old ballad, 'The Wife of Auchtermuchty': 'In the whole range of our ballad literature', wrote William Gunnyon (Illustrations of Scottish History, *1877), 'there is nothing more thoroughly humorous, than The Wife of Auchtermuchty, which is preserved in the Bannatyne Manuscript, and is supposed to be the production of a Sir John Moffat, a "Pope's Knight", and was therefore composed about 1520. It has suffered no alteration or corruption.' It appears in Herd's* Ancient Songs and Ballads *of 1776 (*In Auchtermuchty dwelt a man,/ An husband, as I heard it tawld,/ Quha weil coud tipple out a can,/ And nowther luvit hungir nor cauld: // Till anes it fell upon a day,/ He zokit his plewch upon the plain;/ And schort the storm wald let him stay,/ Sair blew the day with wind and rain./ *etc.) The shorter version with the piquant ending which follows is from a New England 18th-century manuscript of folksongs current during the American Revolution. I have taken the liberty of repairing and completing one or two lines where the words are unintelligible.*

There was a wealthy farmer
As I have heard them Say
As he went out a plowing
Twas on one Stormy day
The wind & Weather
Blew so cold He could no longer Stay
Then he went home unto his wife
And thus to her did Say

'As for you & your Children
You live at home at ease
You do not do any work
But do just as you please
O you shall take your turn
About – or else I'll break
Your bones – Go early in the morning'

So early the next morning
To plow with John she went
She left her Old man warm in bed –
The Children for to tent   *clothe, dress*
He went into the kitchen
To fetch the Child a clout
The old Sow & pigs they did come in
And shat the house about

These pigs they wanted Serving
As you have often seen
They went into the dairy house
And Served them selves with Cream
The cream pots & the milk pans
They rattled all about –
The old Sow did the Churn fling down
Before he got them out

Then he took up the Churndasher
for to drive out the pigs
Some he hit Some he mist
and some he Broke their legs
He drove them out a swearing
Saying death Shall be your Doom –
The old Sow turned her head one Side and
Bit him on the Thumb

Then he went into the Parlour
For to do up his thumb
His Children they were squalling
And crying out for mam
Your mam is gone to plow
& I am almost dead
One fell onto the floor & rolled below the Bed

Then he went in & took his Child
And put it into bed
Then he went up & got his wheel
For to begin his trade
He went out to wash a Clout
And hang the Same to dry
The tow took fire & burnt his wheel
His work went all awry

Then he got tired of womens work
On him that went so cross
He'd go and call his wife in
He'd be no longer nuss
Then he went out like one stark mad –
To call his wife from plow
Young John he was a kissin her
Behind the Barley mow

168 O AN YE WERE DEAD, GUDEMAN *TRADITIONAL*

CHORUS AFTER EACH VERSE

O an ye were dead, gudeman,   *if*
A green turf on your head, gudeman,
I wad bestow my widowhood
Upon a ranton Highlandman.   *boisterous*

There's sax eggs in the pan, gudeman,
There's sax eggs in the pan, gudeman,
There's ane to you, and twa to me,
And three to our John Highlandman.

A sheep-head's in the pot, gudeman.
A sheep-head's in the pot, gudeman;
The flesh to him the broo to me,   *liquid*
An the horns become your brow, gudeman.

Sing round about the fire wi' a rung she ran,   *stick*
An round about the fire wi' a rung she ran,
Your horns shall tie you to the staw,   *stall*
And I shall bang your hide, gudeman.

Burns revised an old song 'I wish that you were dead, goodman' for The Scots Musical Museum *(vol. V, no. 409): it had appeared in Herd's* Ancient and Modern Scottish Songs *in 1776. The theme of a Lowland girl hankering after the supposedly more virile Highlander – expressed in more or less delicate terms – is a common one at the beginning of the 18th century.*

Burns's song 'There was a lad was born in Kyle' is usually sung to this tune although the poet actually set it to the traditional air 'Dainty Davie'. It was probably written in January 1787 in humorous celebration of his birthday, and a note on the MS. of the second stanza states: 'the date of my Bardship's vital existence'.

Robin was a rovin boy,
Rantin, rovin, rantin, rovin,
Robin was a rovin boy,
Rantin' rovin' Robin!

There was a lad was born in Kyle,   *central Ayrshire district*
But what na day o' what na style,
I doubt it's hardly worth the while
To be sae nice wi' Robin.

Our monarch's hindmost year but ane
Was five-and-twenty days begun,
'Twas then a blast o' Janwar' Win   *January Wind*
Blew hansel in on Robin.   *new year or good-luck gift*

The Gossip keekit in his loof,   *friend peered at his hand*
Quo' scho wha lives will see the proof,   *said she*
This waly boy will be nae coof,   *fine boy will be no fool*
I think we'll ca' him Robin.

He'll hae misfortunes great and sma',
But ay a heart aboon them a';
He'll be a credit to us a',
We'll a' be proud o' Robin.

But sure as three times three mak nine,
I see by ilka score and line,   *each*
This chap will dearly like our kin',
So leeze me on thee, Robin.   *I am delighted by*

Guid faith quo' scho I doubt you Sir,
Ye'll gar the lasses lie aspar;   *make the girls lie with legs apart*
But twenty fauts ye may hae waur –
So blessins on thee, Robin.

JOHN ANDERSON MY JO

Lively

John An-der-son my jo, John, When we were first ac-quent; Your

locks were like the ra - ven, Your bon - nie brow was brent; But

now your brow is beld, John, Your locks are like the snaw; But

bless - ings on your fros - ty pow, John An - der - son my jo!

John Anderson my jo, John,
When we were first acquent;
Your locks were like the raven,
Your bonnie brow was brent;   *unwrinkled*
But now your brow is beld, John,
Your locks are like the snaw;
But blessings on your frosty pow,   *head*
John Anderson my jo!

John Anderson my jo, John,
We clamb the hill the gither;
And mony a canty day John,   *pleasant*
We've had wi' ane anither:
Now we maun totter down, John,
And hand in hand we'll go;
And sleep the gither at the foot,
John Anderson my jo.

In the version above Burns has transformed a bawdy traditional song about man's declining sexual powers and an ill-matched couple, into a deeply tender one about the durability of married love – John Anderson and his wife are still sweethearts in old age. A version of the tune appears in the early 17th-century Skene MS and Burns's song was first published in the Scots Musical Museum *of 1790 (vol. III, no. 260) with this note in the index: 'This tune was a piece of Sacred Music in the Roman Catholic times of our Country. – John Anderson is said by tradition to have been town Piper in Kelso.' The Merry Muses of Caledonia has the old version:*

John Anderson, my jo, John,
I wonder what ye mean,
To lie sae lang i' the morning,
And sit sae late at e'en?
Ye'll bleer a' your een, John,
And why do ye so?
Come sooner to your bed at e'en,
John Anderson, my jo.

John Anderson, my jo, John,
When first that ye began,
Ye had as good a tail-tree,
As ony ither man;
But now it's waxen wan, John,
And wrinkles to and fro;
I've twa gae-ups for ae gae-down,
John Anderson, my jo.

I'm backit like a salmon,
I'm breastit like a swan;
My wame it is a down-cod,   *feather pillow*
My middle ye may span:
Frae my tap-knot to my tae, John,
I'm like the new-fa'n snow;
And it's al' for your convenience,
John Anderson, my jo.

O it is a fine thing
To keep out o'er the dyke;
But it's a meikle finer thing,
To see your hurdies fyke;   *buttocks in action*
To see your hurdies fyke, John,
And hit the rising blow;
It's then I like your chanter-pipe,
John Anderson, my jo.

When ye come on before, John,
See that ye do your best;
When ye begin to haud me,
See that ye grip me fast;
See that ye grip me fast, John,
Until that I cry 'Oh!'
Your back shall crack or I do that,
John Anderson, my jo.

John Anderson, my jo, John,
Ye're welcome when ye please;
It's either in the warm bed
Or else aboon the claes:
Or ye shall hae the horns John,
Upon your head to grow;
An that's the cuckold's malison,   *curse*
John Anderson, my jo.

EXILE

meet— se - cure; While— here— I— wan - der,—

prest— with— care, A - long— the— lone - ly— banks of— Ayr.

The gloomy night is gath'ring fast,	'Tis not the surging billow's roar,

The gloomy night is gath'ring fast,
Loud roars the wild, inconstant blast;
Yon murky cloud is foul with rain,
I see it driving o'er the plain;
The hunter now has left the moor,
The scatt'red coveys meet secure;
While here I wander, prest with care,
Along the lonely banks of Ayr.

The Autumn mourns her rip'ning corn
By early Winter's ravage torn;
Across her placid, azure sky,
She sees the scowling tempest fly:
Chill runs my blood to hear it rave,
I think upon the stormy wave,
Where many a danger I must dare,
Far from the bonnie banks of Ayr.

'Tis not the surging billow's roar,
'Tis not that fatal, deadly shore;
Tho' Death in ev'ry shape appear,
The Wretched have no more to fear:
But round my heart the ties are bound,
That heart transpierc'd with many a wound;
These bleed afresh, these ties I tear,
To leave the bonnie banks of Ayr.

Farewell, old Coila's hills and dales,
Her heathy moors and winding vales;
The scenes where wretched Fancy roves,
Pursuing past, unhappy loves!
Farewell, my friends! farewell, my foes!
My peace with these, my love with those –
The bursting tears my heart declare,
Farewell, the bonnie banks of Ayr!

In the autumn of 1786 Burns wrote these words to an old melody, 'The House of Glams' when he believed he was about to emigrate to the West Indies: 'I composed this song' he wrote, 'as I convoyed my chest so far on the road to Greenock, where I was to embark in a few days for Jamaica. I meant it as a farewell Dirge to my native land.' The song was printed in the Scots Musical Museum (no. 284, vol. III), but with an inferior melody. Hewitt's 'Roslin Castle', which Burns admired, had already been published with 'The House of Glams' in the first volume of the Museum. Coila appears in Burns's poem 'The Vision' as the guardian spirit of Kyle, his native district in Ayrshire.

THE SCOTTISH EMIGRANT'S FAREWELL

Moderate

con Ped.

Fare - weel, fare-weel, my na - tive— hame, Thy lone - ly— glens an'

heath - clad— moun - tains, Fare - weel, thy fields o' sto - ried— fame, Thy

leaf - y— shaws an' spark - lin'— foun - tains. Nae mair I'll climb— the—

Pent - lands steep, Nor wan - der— by the Esk's clear— ri - ver; I

seek a hame far o'er the deep, My na-tive land, fare-weel for e-ver.

Fareweel, fareweel, my native hame,
Thy loncly glens an' heathclad mountains,
Fareweel, thy fields o' storied fame,
Thy leafy shaws an' sparklin' fountains.
Nae mair I'll climb the Pentlands steep,
Nor wander by the Esk's clear river;
I seek a hame far o'er the deep,
My native land, fareweel for ever.

Thou land wi' love an' freedom crowned –
In ilk wee cot an' lordly dwellin'
May manly-hearted youths be found,
And maids in ev'ry grace excellin'–
The land where Bruce and Wallace wight
For freedom fought in days o' danger,
Ne'er crouch'd to proud usurpin' might,
But foremost stood, wrong's stern avenger.

Tho' far frae thee, my native shore,
An' toss'd on life's tempestuous ocean;
My heart, aye Scottish to the core,
Shall cling to thee wi' warm devotion.
An' while the wavin' heather grows,
An' onward rows the winding river,
The toast be Scotland's broomy knowes,
Her mountains, rocks, an' glens for ever!

The Edinburgh poet and composer Alexander Hume (1811–59) was self-taught and worked for a time as a cabinet-maker. He began his musical career as a singer, later becoming chorus-master at the Theatre Royal and in his early days was associated with the Glassites, a Scottish religious sect which held that all established religions were against the teaching of Jesus, and every Christian congregation should be self-governing. Hume's arrangement of the Glassite musical manual was his first work as a musician. As well as hymns and psalms Hume wrote many secular lyrics and arranged both these and existing Scottish songs such as Burns's 'Afton Water'. He contributed over 50 items to Lyric Gems of Scotland *which he edited in 1856 having moved to Glasgow in 1855.*

Here a - wa,— there a - wa, wan - der-ing Wil - lie, Here a - wa,—

there a - wa, haud a - wa hame; Come to my bo - som, my ae— on - ly

dear - ie, And tell me thou bring'st me my Wil - lie the same.

Here awa, there awa, wandering Willie,
Here awa, there awa, haud awa hame;
Come to my bosom, my ae only dearie,
And tell me thou bring'st me my Willie the same.

Loud tho' the winter blew cauld on our parting,
'Twas na the blast brought the tear in my e'e:
Welcome now Simmer, and welcome my Willie;
The Simmer to Nature, my Willie to me.

Rest, ye wild storms, in the cave o' your slumbers,
How your dread howling a lover alarms!
Wauken, ye breezes! row gently, ye billows!
And waft my dear Laddie ance mair to my arms.

But oh, if he's faithless, and minds na his Nanie,
Flow still between us, thou wide roaring main:
May I never see it, may I never trow it,
But, dying, believe that my Willie's my ain!

This beautiful tune is in Oswald's Caledonian Pocket Companion *of 1756, and other contemporary collections. The original song Burns modelled his upon is in Herd's* Ancient and Modern Songs *(1776): 'Here awa, there awa, wandering Willie,/ Here awa, there awa, here awa hame;/ Lang have I sought thee, dear have I bought thee,/ Now I have gotten my Willie again.'// Only the first two lines remained when Burns submitted it to publisher George Thomson in 1783, – and he adopted some alterations suggested by 'a committee of taste'. Robert Louis Stevenson was also preoccupied with this saddest of our country tunes: 'I am so besotted', he wrote from Tautira in 1888, 'that I shall put on the back of this my attempt at words to Wandering Willie; if you can conceive at all the difficulty, you will also conceive the vanity with which I regard any kind of result; and whatever mine is like, it has some sense and Burns's has none.'*

Home no more home to me, whither must I wander?
Hunger my driver, I go where I must.
Cold blows the winter wind over hill and heather;
Thick drives the rain, and my roof is in the dust.
Loved of wise men was the shade of my roof-tree.
The true word of welcome was spoken in the door –
Dear days of old, with the faces in the firelight,
Kind folks of old, you come again no more.

Home was home then, my dear, full of kindly faces,
Home was home then, my dear, happy for the child.
Fire and the windows bright glittered on the moorland;
Song, tuneful song, built a palace in the wild.
Now, when day dawns on the brow of the moorland,
Lone stands the house, and the chimney-stone is cold.
Lone let it stand, now the friends are all departed,
The kind hearts, the true hearts, that loved the place of old.

Spring shall come, come again, calling up the moorfowl,
Spring shall bring the sun and rain,
                              bring the bees and the flowers;
Red shall the heather bloom over hill and valley,
Soft flow the stream through the even-flowing hours;
Fair the day shine as it shone on my childhood –
Fair shine the day on the house with open door;
Birds come and cry there and twitter in the chimney –
But I go for ever and come again no more.

THE LAND O' THE LEAL

Moderate

The sun ri-ses bright in France, And fair sets he; But

he has tint the blink he had In my ain coun-trie. It's

no my ain ru-in That weets aye my e'e, But the

dear Ma-rie I left be-hind Wi' sweet bairn-ies three.

con Ped.

The sun rises bright in France,
And fair sets he;
But he has tint the blink he had   *lost the gleam*
In my ain countrie.
It's no my ain ruin
That weets aye my e'e,   *makes me weep so often*
But the dear Marie I left behind
Wi' sweet bairnies three.

The bud comes back to summer,
And the blossom to the tree,
But I win back – oh, never,
To my ain countrie.
Gladness comes to many,
Sorrow comes to me,
As I look o'er the wide ocean
To my ain countrie.

Fu' bienly low'd my ain hearth.   *pleasantly glowed*
And smiled my ain Marie:
Oh! I've left my heart behind
In my ain countrie.
O I'm leal to high heaven,   *loyal*
Which aye was leal to me!
And it's there I'll meet ye a' soon,
Frae my ain countrie.

*Allan Cunningham (1784–1842) was born near Dalswinton
in Dumfriesshire where his father was a friend and neighbour
of Burns. (The twelve-year-old Allan followed the poet's
funeral in 1796.) He was apprenticed at the age of ten to his
stonemason brother but managed to spend a deal of time
reading and writing, later becoming a friend of James Hogg
and Walter Scott. Cunningham wrote many imitation Scots
ballads which were innocently collected as authentic, traditional pieces. Although superintendent of works to the sculp-
tor Francis Legatt Chantrey for thirty years, he was also a
prolific writer. He edited Burns's works (eight volumes) wrote*
Traditional Tales of the Scottish and English Peasantry,
Lives of the most Eminent British Painters, Sculptors and
Architects, *and* Songs of Scotland *which contains his best-
known poem, 'A Wet Sheet and a Flowing Sea'.*

CHORUS AFTER EACH VERSE

My heart's in the Highlands, my heart is not here;
My heart's in the Highlands a-chasing the deer;
A-chasing the wild deer, and following the roe,
My heart's in the Highlands, wherever I go.

Farewell to the Highlands, farewell to the North,
The birth-place of Valour, the country of Worth;
Wherever I wander, wherever I rove,
The hills of the Highlands for ever I love.

Farewell to the mountains high cover'd with snow;
Farewell to the straths and green valleys below:
Farewell to the forests and wild hanging woods;
Farewell to the torrents and loud-pouring floods.

My heart's in the Highlands, my heart is not here;
My heart's in the Highlands a-chasing the deer;
A-chasing the wild deer, and following the roe,
My heart's in the Highlands, wherever I go.

'The first half stanza of this song is old' wrote Burns; 'the rest is mine'.
The original ballad 'The strong walls of Derry' was a favourite of Sir
Walter Scott, who sang it to intimate friends at social occasions,
though only when well-oiled, for the great novelist was considered

'timmer-tun'd', i.e. tone-deaf. The Gaelic air 'Crodh Chailein' or
'Colin's Cattle' (facing page) is now more popular than 'Fàilte na
muisg' or 'The musket salute', below, which Burns chose for the Scots
Musical Museum *(vol. III, no. 259).*

JOY OF MY HEART *SIR HUGH S. ROBERTON*

Moderate

Joy of my heart, Isle of Moo - la! Whi - ther I wan - der East or West,

con Ped.

Wak - ing or dream - ing, thou art near me; Joy of my heart, Isle of Moo - la!

Sing ye o' the Coo - lins of Skye, Of Har - ris, or Eigg, or fair I - o - na.

Joy of my heart, Isle of Mool - a! Whi - ther I wan - der East or West,

D.S. al Fine

Wak- ing or dream - ing,   thou art near me;   Joy of my heart, Isle of   Moo - la!

Joy of my heart, Isle of Moola!	*Eilean mo chrìdh Muile ghràdhach,*
Whither I wander East or West,	*Siubhlam sear no siubhlam siar,*
Waking or dreaming, thou art near me;	*Mhoch 's an ciaradh tha thu làmh rium,*
Joy of my heart, Isle of Moola!	*Eilean mo chrìdh Muile ghràdhach.*

Sing ye o' the Coolins of Skye,
Of Harris, or Eigg, or fair Iona.

Luaidhibhse mu'n Chuilionn ghreannach
Eig' 's na Hearradh 's I nan gràsan.

Joy of my heart, Isle of Moola!
Whither I wander East or West,
Waking or dreaming, thou art near me;
Joy of my heart, Isle of Moola!

Eilean mo chrìdh Muile ghràdhach,
Siubhlam sear no siubhlam siar,
Mhoch 's an ciaradh tha thu làmh rium,
Eilean mo chrìdh Muile ghràdhach.

Peat and heather! how you call me,
Little wee bothan by the hillside.

Mòine 's fraoch gam ghairm gu caomh
'S am bothan gaoil is rogha fàrdaich.

Joy of my heart, Isle of Moola!
Whither I wander East or West,
Waking or dreaming, thou art near me;
Joy of my heart, Isle of Moola!

Eilean mo chrìdh Muile ghràdhach,
Siubhlam sear no siubhlam siar,
Mhoch 's an ciaradh tha thu làmh rium,
Eilean mo chrìdh Muile ghràdhach.

Kindly hearts are waiting to cheer me,
Welcoming arms are there to hold me.

Sud far bheil na cairdean coibhneil,
Chuireas aoibh orm le'm fàilte.

Joy of my heart, Isle of Moola!
Whither I wander East or West,
Waking or dreaming, thou art near me;
Joy of my heart, Isle of Moola!

Eilean mo chrìdh Muile ghràdhach,
Siubhlam sear no siubhlam siar,
Mhoch 's an ciaradh tha thu làmh rium,
Eilean mo chrìdh Muile ghràdhach.

These verses about Mull come from Roberton's Songs of the Isles, Gaelic melodies to which he put new words. Some may be sentimental and inappropriate to the tunes' traditions, but many remain great favourites. Hugh Stevenson Roberton (1874–1952) was founder-conductor of the legendary Glasgow Orpheus Choir, begun in 1905: the choir's distinctive style was immensely popular in Britain, Europe and North America, and Roberton (later Sir Hugh) wrote songs for them, as well as arranging Scottish folkmusic and psalm tunes.

CHI MI NA MOR-BHEANNA *JOHN CAMERON*

Broadly

O, chì, chì mi na mòr-bhean-na; O, chì, chì mi na còrr-bhean-na; Ho - ro! chì mi na coir-each-an,

Chì mi na sgòr-an fo cheò.——— Chì mi gun dàil an t-àit-e 'san d'rug-adh mi;

Cuir - ear orm fàilt-e 'sa chàn-ain a thuig-eas mi; Gheibh mi ann aoidh ag-us

D.C. al Fine

grádh___ 'nuair ruig - eam, Nach reic - inn air tunn - ach - an òir.___

CHORUS, THEN SOLO

O, chì, chì mi na mòr-bheanna;
O, chì, chì mi na còrr-bheanna;
Horo! chì mi na coireachan,
Chì mi na sgòran fo cheò.

Chì mi gun dàil an t-àite 'san d'rugadh mi;
Cuirear orm fàilte 'sa chànain a thuigeas mi;
Gheibh mi ann aoidh agus gràdh 'nuair ruigeam,
Nach reicinn air tunnachan òir.

Chì mi ann coilltean; chì mi ann doireachan;
Chì mi ann màghan bàna is torraiche;
Chì mi na fèidh air làr nan coireachan,
Falaicht' an trusgan de cheò,

Beanntaicheann àrda is àillidh leacainnean;
Sluagh ann an còmhuidh is còire cleachdainnean;
'S aotrom mo cheum a' leum g'am faicinn;
'Us fanaidh mi tacan le deòin.

Fàilt' air na gorm mheallaibh tholmach, thulchanach;
Fàilt' air na còrr-bheannaibh mòra, mulanach;
Fàilt' air na coilltean, is fàilt' air na h-uile,
O! 's sona bhi 'fuireach 'nan còir.

John Cameron was a native of Ballachulish. His song, set to an old Highland melody, is best known in the translation by Malcom Macfarlane who edited Songs of the Highlands. *Sometimes known as 'Hail to the mighty Bens' it is popular with the regimental pipe bands.*

CHORUS AFTER EACH VERSE

Hoo, O! Soon shall I see them, O;
Hee, O! See them , O see them, O;
Horo! Soon shall I see them,
The mist-covered mountains of home.

There shall I visit the place of my birth;
And they'll give me a welcome,
                        the warmest on earth;
All so loving and kind full of music and mirth,
In the sweet-sounding language of home.

There I shall gaze on the mountains again;
On the fields and the woods
                        and the burns in the glen;
And away 'mong the corries,
                        beyond human ken,
In the haunts of the deer I shall roam.

There I'll converse with the hard-headed father;
And there I shall jest
                        with the kind-hearted mother,
O, light is my heart as I turn my steps thither,
The ever-dear precincts of home.

Hail! to the mountains with summits of blue;
To the glens with their meadows
                        of sunshine and dew;
To the women and men ever constant and true,
Ever ready to welcome one home.

MINGULAY BOAT SONG

Hill you ho, boys; let her go, boys; Bring her head round, now all— to - ge - ther. Hill you

ho, boys: let her go, boys; Sail - ing home,— home to Min - gu - lay. What care

we tho' white— the Minch is? What care we for wind— or wea - ther? Let her

D.S.

go, boys! ev - 'ry inch is Wear - ing home, home to Min - gu - lay.

Hill you ho, boys; let her go, boys;
Bring her head round, now all together.
Hill you ho, boys: let her go, boys;
Sailing home, home to Mingulay.

What care we tho' white the Minch is?
What care we for wind or weather?
Let her go, boys! ev'ry inch is
Wearing home, home to Mingulay.

Hill you ho, boys; let her go, boys;
Bring her head round, now all together.
Hill you ho, boys: let her go, boys;
Sailing home, home to Mingulay.

Wives are waiting on the bank, or
Looking seaward from the heather;
Pull her round boys! and we'll anchor,
Ere the sun sets at Mingulay.

Hill you ho, boys; let her go, boys;
Bring her head round, now all together.
Hill you ho, boys: let her go, boys;
Sailing home, home to Mingulay.

Sir Hugh Roberton (1874–1952) was conductor of the famous
Orpheus Choir of Glasgow, for which he made many choral arrange-
ments of Scots songs. He also published Songs of the Isles *(1950), a*
collection of traditional tunes for which he invented English words.
'Mairi's Wedding' (the Lewis Bridal Song), 'Westering Home' and the
'Mingulay Boat Song' were all popularized by Roberton and they
remain perennial favourites. The remote, barren island of Mingulay
lies to the south of Barra in the Western Isles. Sometimes referred to
as 'the nearer St Kilda', it was a crofting and fishing community of
about 160 people until 1912. Isolation, infertile land, lack of a
proper landing place and the absentee landlord problems familiar to
the Western Isles and Highlands, resulted in a gradual disintegration
of Mingulay's culture. The process of voluntary evacuation began in
1907 with land raids by the impoverished crofters to the neighbour-
ing island of Vatersay, and Mingulay is now completely deserted. But
summer visitors to Barra regularly brave the two-hour journey in
exposed seas from Castlebay to Mingulay, inspired by Roberton's
evocative but sentimental song, which has no connection with either
the island or its people.

Expressive

O— ro - wan tree, O ro - wan tree, thou'lt aye be dear to me!— En -

con Ped.

twin'd thou art wi' mo - ny ties o' hame and in - fan - cy. Thy

leaves were aye the first o' Spring, thy flow'rs the Sim - mer's pride;— There

was nae sic a bon - nie tree in a' the coun - try side; O— ro - wan tree!

O rowan tree, O rowan tree,
      thou'lt aye be dear to me!
Entwin'd thou art wi' mony ties
      o' hame and infancy.
Thy leaves were aye the first o' Spring,
      thy flow'rs the Simmer's pride;
There was nae sic a bonnie tree
      in a' the country side;
O rowan tree!

How fair wert thou in simmer time
      wi' a' thy clusters white;
How rich and gay thy Autumn dress,
      wi' berries red and bright;
On thy fair stem were mony names,
      which now nae mair I see,
But they're engraven on my heart,
      forgot they ne'er can be.
O rowan tree!

We sat aneath thy spreading shade,
      the bairnies round thee ran,
They pu'd thy bonnie berries red,
      and necklaces they strang;
My mither, Oh! I see her still,
      she smiles our sports to see,
Wi' little Jeanie on her lap, and Jamie at her knee.
O rowan tree!

Oh! there arose my father's prayer,
      in holy evening's calm,
How sweet was then my mither's voice
      in the martyr's psalm!
Now a' are gane! We meet nae mair
      aneath the rowan tree,
But hallowed thoughts around thee turn
      o' hame and infancy.
O rowan tree!

Carolina Oliphant, Lady Nairne, was the daughter of Lawrence Oliphant of Gask, a staunch Jacobite, who had followed Prince Charlie through the '45 and who always referred to King George as 'The Elector of Hanover'. She wrote many romantic Jacobite songs, and 'purified' a lot of traditional material, but some Lady Nairne favourites are originals, like 'The Rowan Tree' and 'The Auld Hoose', which look back nostalgically to childhood and the simple pleasures of (aristocratic) country life. Circumstances prevented her marriage until she was over forty, and both her husband and her only child predeceased her, which may account for the religious austerity of her old age – though none of this is evident in her poetry.

FAREWELL TO FIUNARY *DR NORMAN MACLEOD*

The wind is fair, the day is fine And swift-ly, swift-ly runs the time; The

boat is float-ing on the tide That wafts me off from Fiu-na-ry.

We must up and be a-way! We must up and be a-way!

We must up and be a-way! Fare-well, fare-well to Fiu-na-ry.

The wind is fair, the day is fine
And swiftly, swiftly runs the time;
The boat is floating on the tide
That wafts me off from Fiunary.

We must up and be away!
We must up and be away!
We must up and be away!
Farewell, farewell to Fiunary.

A thousand, thousand tender ties –
Awake this day my plaintive sighs;
My heart within me almost dies
At thought of leaving Fiunary.

With pensive steps I've often strolled
Where Fingal's castle stood of old,
And listened while the shepherds told
The legend tales of Fiunary.

I've often paused at close of day
Where Ossian sang his martial lay,
And viewed the sun's departing ray,
Wand'ring o'er Dun-Fiunary.

Aultan Caluch's gentle stream,
That murmurs sweetly through the green,
What happy, joyful days I've seen,
Beside the banks of Fiunary.

Farewell ye hills of storm and snow,
The wild resorts of deer and roe;
In peace the heath-cock long may crow,
Along the banks of Fiunary.

'Tis not the hills nor woody vales
Alone my joyless heart bewails;
But a mournful group this day remains
Within the Manse of Fiunary.

Can I forget Glen Turret's name?
Farewell, dear father, best of men:
May heaven's joys with thee remain
Within the Manse of Fiunary.

Tha'n latha math, 's an soirbheas ciùin;
Tha'n uine 'ruith, 's an t-àm dhuinn dlùth;
Tha'm bàt' 'gam fheitheamh fo a siùil,
Gu m'thoirt a null o Fionnairidh.

Eirich agus tiugainn, O!
Eirigh agus tiugainn, O!
Eirigh agus tiugainn, O!
Mo shoraidh slàn le Fionnairidh.

Tha iomadh mìle ceangal blàth
Mar shaighdean annam fèin an sàs;
Mo chridhe 'n impis a bhi sgàint'
A chionn 'bhi 'fàgail Fionnairidh.

Bu tric a ghabh mi sgrìob leam fhèin
Mu'n cuairt air lùchairt Fhìnn an trèin;
'S a dh'èisd mi sgeulachdan na Fèinn'
'Gan cur an cèill am Fionnairidh.

Bu tric a sheall mi feasgar Màirt
Far am biodh Oisean 'seinn a dhàin;
A' coimhead grèin aig ioma tràth
'Dol seach gach là's mi'm Fionnairidh.

Beannachd le beanntaibh mo ghaoil
Far am faigh mi'm fiadh le 'laogh,–
Gu ma fad' an coileach-fraoich
A' glaodhaich ann am Fionnairidh.

Ach cha'n iad glinn us beanntan àrd'
A lot mo chrìdh 's a rinn mo chràdh,
Ach an diugh na tha fo phràmh,
An teach mo ghràidh am Fionnairidh.

Beannachd le athair mo ghràidh;
Bidh mi cuimhneach ort gu bràth;
Ghuidhinn sonas agus àgh
Do'n t-sean fhear bhàn am Fionnairidh.

Am feum mi siubhal uait gun dàil?
Na siùil tha togte ris a bhàt' –
Soraidh slàn le tìr mo ghràidh,
'Us slàn, gu bràth le Fionnairidh!

Mother! a name to me so dear,
Must I, must I leave thy care,
And try a world that's full of snares
Far, far from thee and Fiunary?

Brother of my love, farewell –
Sister, all thy griefs conceal –
Thy tears suppress, thy sorrows quell,
Be happy while at Fiunary.

Archibald! my darling child,
May Heaven thy infant footsteps guide,
Should I return, Oh, may I find
Thee smiling still at Fiunary.

Oh! must I leave these happy scenes?
See, they spread the flapping sails,
Adieu! adieu! my native plains;
Farewell, farewell to Fiunary!

This song was written by Dr Norman Macleod (1783–1862), a son of the beautifully-situated manse at Fiunary in Morvern, who was known as 'Caraid nan Gaidheal' or Friend of the Gaels, in recognition of his work for education and famine relief in the Highlands. His father, also Norman, was a Skyeman who was appointed to the parish by the Duke of Argyll on account of his staunch presbyterianism and Hanoverian sympathies: he was instrumental in reconciling the people of Morvern to the final collapse of their Jacobite hopes, and leading them from episcopalianism to the established church. Of the elder Norman's sixteen children only two sons reached manhood, one of them the author of these popular verses. 'Farewell to Fiunary' was written on the young man's departure to Glasgow University and it used to be sung at social gatherings in the West Highlands as a parting song, in the manner of 'Auld Lang Syne' – 'Fiunary' to the Gael being synonymous with 'home'. 'Caraid nan Gaidheal' became minister of St Columba's in Glasgow, and a distinguished dynasty of churchmen, politicians and teachers has followed him to the present day (the Very Rev G.F., Baron Fiunary founded the Iona Community in 1938). The tune of 'Farewell to Fiunary' is much older than Dr Macleod's verses, and originally accompanied Allan MacDougal's song 'Irinn oirinn u horo'. This bard, who was better known as 'Ailean Dall' or Blind Allan, was born in Glencoe in 1750.

COME ALL YE!

A.GRAY after I.KAY

THE PIPER O' DUNDEE

The pi - per came to our town, To our town, to our town, The

pi - per came to our town, And he played bon - ni - lie. He

played a spring, the laird to please, A spring brent new frae yont the seas; And

he then gae his bag a wheeze, And played a - ni - ther key. *And was - na he a ro - gie, A*

D.S.

ro - gie, a ro - gie, And was - na he a ro - gie, The pi - per o' Dun - dee?

CHORUS AFTER EVERY VERSE

The piper came to our town,
To our town, to our town,
The piper came to our town,
And he played bonnilie.
He played a spring, the laird to please,   *dance tune*
A spring brent new frae yont the seas;   *brand new*
And he then gae his bag a wheeze,
And played anither key.

And wasna he a rogie,
A rogie, a rogie,
And wasna he a rogie,
The piper o' Dundee?

He played 'The Welcome owre the Main',
And 'Ye'se be fou and I'se be fain',
And 'Auld Stuarts back again',
Wi' muckle mirth and glee.
He played 'The Kirk', he played 'The Queen',
'The Mullin Dhu', and 'Chevalier',
And 'Lang away, but welcome here',
Sae sweet, sae bonnilie.

It's some gat swords, and some gat nane,
And some were dancing mad their lane,
And mony a vow o' weir was taen   *declaration of war*
That night at Amulrie.
There was Tullibardine and Burleigh,
And Struan, Keith, and Ogilvie,
And brave Carnegie, wha but he,
The piper o' Dundee?

The hero of this Jacobite song is supposed to have been Carnegie of Phinhaven, celebrated as the best flyer from the field of Sherriffmuir during the Jacobite revolt of 1715. The ballad about that battle mentions: The laird of Phinaven, who sware to be even/ Wi' ony general and peer o' them a', man.// Whether Carnegie was a piper is not clear but there are certainly reports of a Dundee piper who got himself into trouble playing subversive tunes. All those mentioned in the song date from the 18th century or earlier. Amulrie is a village in Perthshire.

THE DEIL CAM FIDDLIN THRO' THE TOWN

The deil cam fiddlin thro' the town,   *devil*
And danc'd awa wi' th'Exciseman,
And ilka wife cries, Auld Mahoun, *the devil (Mohammed)*
I wish you luck o' the prize, man!

The deil's awa, the deil's awa,
The deil's awa wi' th'Exciseman!
He's danc'd awa, he's danc'd awa,
He's danc'd awa wi' th'Exciseman!

We'll mak our maut and we'll brew our drink,   *ale*
We'll laugh, sing, and rejoice, man;
And mony braw thanks to the meikle black deil,
That danc'd awa wi' th'Exciseman.

The deil's awa, the deil's awa,
The deil's awa wi' th'Exciseman!
He's danc'd awa, he's danc'd awa,
He's danc'd awa wi' th'Exciseman!

There's threesome reels, there's foursome reels,
There's hornpipes and strathspeys, man,
But the aye best dance e'er cam to the Land
Was, the deil's awa wi' th'Exciseman.

The deil's awa, the deil's awa,
The deil's awa wi' th'Exciseman!
He's danc'd awa, he's danc'd awa,
He's danc'd awa wi' th'Exciseman!

This song dates from Burns's days as an exciseman. As a young man
he had scorned the Excise in its business of curbing illegal whisky
stills; now he could laugh at himself and his unpopular employ-
ment. The poet sang the song at an Excise dinner but it was
probably written while he was watching the movements of the
crew of a stranded smuggler on the Solway. His colleague had gone
to Dumfries for reinforcements and Burns was left for several
hours pacing the marshes. The song was enclosed in a letter to J.
Levan, General Supervisor of the Excise, with these words of
introduction: 'Mr Mitchell mentioned to you a ballad, which I
composed and sung at one of his excise dinners: here it is . . . If
you honour my ballad by making it one of your charming bon
vivant *effusions, it will secure it undoubted celebrity.' It is no. 399*
of the Scots Musical Museum *(1792).*

ISLAND SPINNING SONG

Hull- a- mack- a- doo, Hoo- ro- va- hee, Hoo- ro- va- hin- da, Hee- ro- va- hin- da,

Hull- a- mack- a- doo, Hoo- ro- va- hee, O— dick- o- deck- o- dan— dy.

When will some- one— come to me? Will he come by— land or sea?

Will he my own— lo- ver be? O— tell me tru- ly, wheel, O.

Hull-a-mack-a-doo,
Hoo-ro-va-hee,
Hoo-ro-va-hin-da,
Hee-ro-va-hin-da,
Hull-a-mack-a-doo,
Hoo-ro-va-hee,
O dick-o-deck-o-dan-dy.

When will someone come to me?
Will he come by land or sea?
Will he my own lover be?
O tell me truly, wheel, O.

Wheel o' fate, what is't you say?
This year, next, or ne'er a day?
When will wooer come my way?
O, tell me truly, wheel, O.

Be he dark or be he fair,
Shy or bold or debonair,
Ribbons braw will deck my hair
To meet and greet my true love.

Sir Hugh Roberton included this traditional Gaelic tune (taken from the singing of Donalda Macleod of Glasgow) in his popular collection Songs of the Isles. *The original Gaelic words are by Angus Robertson but these English words are strictly Roberton.*

Moderate

Chaidh na fir a Sgath - abh - aig. Fàill___ ill, O - ho - rò!

Tha'n là'n diu fuar ac'. O hì, ho - rionn o - hò,

Hi ri rì ho - ro___ gù, Fàill ill O - ho - rò.

VERSE: Chaidh na fir a Sgathabhaig.
REFRAIN: Fàill ill, Ohorò!
VERSE: Tha'n là'n diu fuar ac'.
REFRAIN: O hì, horionn ohò,
Chorus: Hi ri rì horo gù,
       Fàill ill Ohorò.

Chaidh fear mo thighe-s' ann;
Fàill ill, Ohorò!
Caol mhala gun ghruaman;
O hì, horionn ohò,
Hi ri rì horo gù,
Fàill ill Ohorò.

Sealgair an ròin teillich thu;
Fàill ill, Ohorò!
Is na h-eilide ruaidhe;
O hì, horionn ohò,
Hi ri rì horo gù,
Fàill ill Ohorò.

Is na circeige duinne thu,
Fàill ill, Ohorò!
Nì a nead's a luachair.
O hì, horionn ohò,
Hi ri rì horo gù,
Fàill ill Ohorò.

(1. The men have gone to Scavaig (Refrain) for them this day is cold (Refrain and Chorus) 2. The goodman of my house went there; he of the slender eyebrows, showing no frown. // 3. Hunter of the blub-cheeked seal art thou, and of the red hind, // 4. and of the little brown hen that makes her nest among the rushes. //)

This song comes from Minginish on the west coast of Skye and Loch Scavaig is a sea loch – an abundant fishing ground – situated some miles to the south. Frances Tolmie (1840–1926) who remembered this song from her childhood, was one of the foremost of Gaelic folklore and folksong experts. She was bilingual and faithfully noted down both words and tunes of a large number of songs from her native Skye, and her collection is authentic and realistic, unlike the 'drawing-room' arrangements of the more fashionable and famous collector of Hebridean songs, Marjory Kennedy-Fraser, who had no Gaelic. Many island songs are communal work songs, and this one would have accompanied the waulking, or shrinking, of handwoven tweed – the final stage in the process. A dozen or so women would assemble for a waulking. They would sit round a large table and toss and beat the cloth (soaked in urine to soften the wool and to fix the dye) singing rhythmically all the while. The pattern was usually a solo verse of one line followed by a meaningless refrain which was followed by a chorus which everyone joined in. Some of the waulking songs were very long, and there was often improvisation.

D. S. for verses 2 – 6

REPEAT CHORUS AFTER EACH VERSE

Wha'll buy caller herrin'?   *fresh herring*
They're bonnie fish and halesome farin';   *wholesome food*
Buy my caller herrin',
New drawn frae the Forth.

When ye are sleeping on your pillows,
Dreamt ye aught o' our puir fellows,
Darkling as they face the billows,
A' to fill our woven willows.

Noo a' ye lads at herrin' fishing,
Costly vamping, dinner dressing,
Sole or turbot, how distressing,
Fine folks scorn shoals o' blessing.

And when the creel o' herrin' passes,
Ladies, clad in silk and laces,
Gather in their braw pelisses,
Cast their heads an' screw their faces.

Noo neebour's wives, come tent my tellin',   *heed*
When the bonnie fish ye're sellin',
At a word aye be your dealin',
Truth will stand when a'thing's failin'.

Wha'll buy caller herrin'?
They're bonnie fish and halesome farin';
Buy my caller herrin',
New drawn frae the Forth.

Like Robert Burns, Lady Nairne frequently rewrote old songs – especially if she considered the words indelicate – but this one, like 'The Rowan Tree' and 'The Auld Hoose' is completely original. She used a melody by Nathaniel Gow (1766–1831), mentioned in some versions: . . . Ye can tip the spring fu' tightly;/ Spite o' tauntin', flauntin', flingin'; Gow has set you a' a-singing//. Like his famous father Niel, he was a fine composer, and an important figure in the musical life of Edinburgh.

Is there for honest poverty
That hings his head, an' a' that?   *hangs*
The coward slave, we pass him by –
We dare be poor for a' that!
For a' that, an' a' that,
Our toils obscure, an' a' that,
The rank is but the guinea's stamp,
The man's the gowd for a' that. –   *gold*

What tho' on hamely fare we dine,
Wear hoddin grey an' a' that.   *homespun*
Gie fools their silks, and knaves their wine –
A man's a man for a' that.
For a' that, an' a' that,
Their tinsel show, an' a' that;
The honest man, tho' e'er sae poor,
Is king o' men for a' that.

Ye see yon birkie ca'd a lord,   *conceited fellow*
Wha struts, and stares, an' a' that,
Tho' hundreds worship at his word,
He's but a coof for a' that.   *a fool*
For a' that, an' a' that,
His ribband, star, an' a' that,
The man of independent mind,
He looks and laughs at a' that. –

A prince can mak a belted knight,
A marquis, duke, an' a' that,
But an honest man's aboon his might,   *above*
Gude faith he mauna fa' that!   *must not lay claim to*
For a' that, an' a' that,
Their dignities, an' a' that,
The pith o' Sense, and pride o' Worth,
Are higher rank than a' that.

Then let us pray that come it may,
As come it will for a' that,
That Sense and Worth, o'er a' the earth
Shall bear the gree, an' a' that. –   *come off best*
For a' that, an' a' that,
It's comin yet for a' that,
That man to man the warld o'er,
Shall brothers be for a' that.

This is Burns's most famous democratic political song. 'In "Scots wha hae"', wrote Thomas Crawford, 'the concept of nationalism (earlier often present in a Jacobite form) is completely fused with that of freedom; and in the fifth stanza of "Is there for honest poverty?" it has been transcended in a blending of internationalism with the revolutionary idea of fraternity'. The ideas are akin to those of Thomas Paine whose essay 'The rights of man' had been published a year or two before. The tune, 'For a' that, an' a' that', has been popular since the mid-18th century: it appeared in Bremner's Scots Reels *(1759) and various other collections and Burns had used it earlier in a similarly defiant song 'I am a bard, of no regard'. It also appears in the* Scots Musical Museum *(vol. III, no. 290) with these verses: Tho' womens' minds like winter winds/ May shift and turn and a' that,/ The noblest breast adores them maist,/ A consequence I draw that./ For a' that, and a' that,/ And twice as meikle as a' that,/ The bonny lass that I lo'e best/ She'll be my ain for a' that.//*

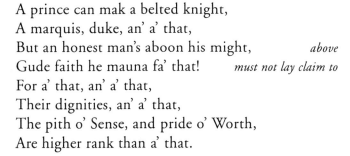

Slow

I'm wear - in' a - wa', John, Like snaw - wreaths in thaw,— John, I'm

con Ped.

wear - in' a - wa'— To the land— o' the Leal. There's

nae sor - row there, John, There's nei - ther cauld nor care,— John, The

day is aye— fair— In the land— o' the Leal.

I'm wearin' awa', John,
Like snaw-wreaths in thaw, John,
I'm wearin' awa'
To the land o' the Leal.

faithful

There's nae sorrow there, John,
There's neither cauld nor care , John,
The day is aye fair
In the land o' the Leal.

Our bonnie bairn's there, John,   *child*
She was baith gude and fair, John,
And oh! we grudged her sair
To the land o' the Leal.

But sorrow's sel' wears past, John,   *sorrow itself*
And joy is comin' fast, John, –
The joy that's aye to last
In the land o' the Leal.

Sae dear's that joy was bought, John,
Sae free the battle fought, John,
That sinfu' men e'er brought
To the land o' the Leal.

Oh dry your tearfu' e'e, John,
My soul langs to be free, John,
And angels beckon me
To the land o' the Leal.

Oh, haud ye leal and true, John!
Your day is wearin' through, John;
And I will welcome you
To the land o' the Leal.

Now fair ye weel, my ain John,
This warld's cares are vain, John;
We'll meet and aye be fain   *loving*
In the land o' the Leal.

Lady Nairne (nee Carolina Oliphant) wrote this song in 1798 to console her friend, Mrs Campbell Colquhoun of Killermont, after the death of her first child. Mrs Colquhoun's grief was so intense that she had a wax cast made of the baby and Carolina sent her the verses hoping that they would help her friend come to terms with her loss. As usual, the retiring Lady Nairne requested anonymity regarding authorship – she used the pseudonym B.B. for Mrs Bogan of Bogan, when publishing her songs – and for many years it was thought that Burns had written 'that deathless hymn, cradle-croon of Scotland's children' (Jean instead of John throughout). He certainly used the tune, 'Hey Tutti Taitie', on two occasions, using faster tempi to startlingly different effect: 'Landlady, count the lawin', a cheerful drinking song which Burns expanded from traditional fragments, and the martial 'Scots Wha Hae wi' Wallace Bled'. But the tune can be found earlier, in McGibbon's Scots Tunes *and Oswald's* Caledonian Pocket Companion, *Bk. III. (A 'tutti-taiti(e)', according to the* Concise Scots Dictionary, *is an exclamation representing the sound of a trumpet. A 'lawin' is the bill or reckoning.)*

AMATING GRACE

Amazing grace! how sweet the sound
That saved a wretch like me!
I once was lost, but now am found,
Was blind, but now I see.

'Twas grace that taught my heart to fear,
And grace my fears relieved;
How precious did that grace appear
The hour I first believed.

Through many dangers, toils, and snares
I have already come;
'Tis grace hath brought me safe thus far,
And grace will lead me home.

The lord has promised good to me,
His word my hope secures;
He will my shield and portion be
As long as life endures.

Yes, when this heart and flesh shall fail,
And mortal life shall cease,
I shall possess within the veil
A life of joy and peace.

'Amazing Grace' was recorded by the Royal Scots Dragoon Guards as an album-filler and became 'Top of the Pops' for nine weeks. The tune is still immensely popular, but the actual hymn is more often found in the hymn books of America than this country. It was written by an Englishman, John Newton (1725–1807), who was sent to the navy at the age of eleven. Newton lived, according to his own account, a godless life of dissipation, and having deserted at twenty-two (for which he was flogged) became captain of a ship engaging in the slave trade. Three years later when he was crossing the Atlantic a violent storm erupted, and after nine hours manning the pumps and another seventeen terrifying hours at the wheel, he underwent a dramatic conversion. He gave up the slave trade and spent nine years training for ordination in the Anglican Church. This hymn, one of many Newton wrote, was first published in 1779. The folk tune to which it was set came to America from Scotland in the 18th century.

CHORUS AFTER EVERY VERSE

Should auld acquaintance be forgot,   *old*
And never brought to mind?
Should auld acquaintance be forgot,
And auld lang syne?   *long ago*

For auld lang syne, my jo,   *sweetheart*
For auld lang syne,
We'll tak a cup o' kindness yet,
For auld lang syne.

And surely ye'll be your pint stowp!   *measure*
And surely I'll be mine!
And we'll tak a cup o' kindness yet,
For auld lang syne.

We twa hae run about the braes,
And pou'd the gowans fine;   *pulled the wild flowers*
But we've wandered mony a weary fitt,   *foot*
Sin auld lang syne.

We twa hae paidl'd in the burn,   *paddled*
Frae morning sun till dine;   *dinner-time*
But seas between us braid hae roar'd   *broad*
Sin auld lang syne.

And there's a hand, my trusty fiere!   *companion*
And gie's a hand o' thine!
And we'll tak a right gude-willie-waught,   *cordial drink*
For auld lang syne.

'The air is but mediocre', wrote Burns to his publisher, George Thomson, 'but the following song, the old Song of the olden times, and which has never been in print, not even in manuscript, until I took it down from an old man's singing; is enough to recommend any air'. He was speaking about the tune printed below. Thomson adopted another, if similar, tune from the Scots Musical Museum *(vol. IV, no. 394),'I fee'd a man at Martinmas', for his 1799 collection of* Scotish Airs. *It is sung today in different languages all round the world, but especially on Hogmanay. Although many think the words are by Burns he himself denied authorship in a letter to Mrs Dunlop of 7 December 1788. '. . . Is not the Scots phrase, "Auld lang syne" singularly expressive. – There is an old song and tune which has often thrilled thro' my soul . . . Light be the turf on the breast of the heaven-inspired Poet who composed this glorious fragment! There is more of the fire of native genius in it, than in half a dozen of modern English Bacchanalians.'*

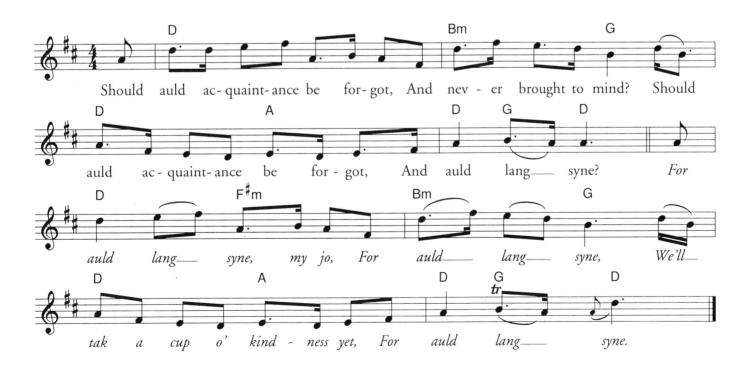

INDEX OF TITLES

AND FIRST LINES

A

A FAIRY LULLABY 158
A HIGHLAND LAD MY LOVE WAS BORN 92
A Highland lad my love was born 93
A MAN'S A MAN FOR A' THAT 206
About Yule, when the wind blew cool, 95
AE FOND KISS 130
Ae fond kiss, and then we sever! 131
AIR FEASGAR CIUIN CEITEIN 34
Air feasgar ciùin Cèitein 35
Ally, bally, ally, bally bee 161
AMAZING GRACE 210
Amazing grace! how sweet the sound 211
An' Charlie, he's my darling, 49
AN COINEACHAN 158
An eartly nourris sits and sings, 116
As I cam o'er the Cairney mount, 103
AS I CAME O'ER THE CAIRNEY MOUNT 102
As I was walking all alane, 77
AULD LANG SYNE 214
AY, WAUKIN, O 28
Ay, waukin, O, 29

B

Being pursu'd by the dragoons, 111
Bheir mi òro bhan ó, 107
Bonnie Charlie's noo awa', 51
BONNIE DUNDEE 14
BONNIE GEORGE CAMPBELL 83
Bonnie lassie, will ye go – *Burns's version* 37

BONNY BARBARA ALLAN 122
Bonny lassic, will yc go, – *traditional version* 37
By yon bonnie banks and by yon bonnie braes, 133
By yon castle wa' at the close of the day, 43

C

CA' THE YOWES TO THE KNOWES 32
Ca' the yowes to the knowes – *Burns's first version* 33
Ca' the yowes to the knowes, – *later version* 33
Cagaran, cagaran, cagaran gaolach, 157
CAGARAN GAOLACH 156
CALLER HERRIN' 204
CHAIDH NA FIR A SGATHABHAIG 202
Chaidh na fir a Sgathabhaig 203
CHARLIE, HE'S MY DARLING 49
CHARLIE IS MY DARLING 48
CHI MI NA MOR–BHEANNA 186
CHILD IN THE MANGER 163
Child in the manger, Infant of Mary; 163
COME O'ER THE STREAM, CHARLIE 46
Come o'er the stream, Charlie, dear
            Charlie, dear Charlie 47
Cope sent a challenge frae Dunbar, 9
Corn Riggs Are Bonny 114
CORN RIGS 112
COULTER'S CANDY 160

D

DAINTY DAVIE 110
Dh'fhàg mi'n so na shìneadh e, 159

DUNCAN GRAY   18
Duncan Gray cam here to woo,   19

E

EILEAN MO CHRIDH   185
Eilean mo chrìdh Muile ghràdhach,   185
ERISKAY LOVE LILT   106

F

Fareweel, fareweel, my native hame,   177
FAREWELL TO FIUNARY   192
Farewell, ye dungeons dark and strong   91
FINE FLOWERS IN THE VALLEY   98
FLOW GENTLY, SWEET AFTON   108
Flow gently, sweet Afton,
            among thy green braes,   109

G

GILDEROY   120
Gilderoy was a bonny Boy,   121
GLENOGIE   66
GRADH GEAL MO CHRIDH   106
GREEN GROW THE RASHES, O   100
Green grow the rashes O – *polite version*   101
Green grow the rashes, O – *rude version*   101

H

Here awa, there awa, wandering Willie,   179
Hie upon Hielands, and laigh upon Tay,   83
HIGHLAND LADDIE   44
Hill you ho, boys; let her go, boys   189
HO RO MO NIGHEAN DONN
            BHOIDHEACH   20
Ho rò, mo nighean donn bhòidheach,   21
HO-RO MY NUT-BROWN MAIDEN   21
Ho-ro my nut-brown maiden,   21
Home no more home to me,   179
Hoo, O! Soon shall I see them, O   187
How blyth was I each morn to see   65
Hull-a-mack-a-doo   201

HUSH YE, MY BAIRNIE   157
Hush ye, my bairnie, my bonnie wee lammie;   157

I

I am my mammy's ae bairn,   137
I left my darling lying here,   159
I LOVE MY LOVE IN SECRET   58
If thou'lt play me fair play,   45
I'M O'ER YOUNG TO MARRY YET   136
I'm wearin' awa', John,   209
In June, when broom in bloom was seen,   147
In Norway land there lived a maid.   117
Is there for honest poverty   207
ISLAND SPINNING SONG   200
It fell on a day, a bonny simmer day,   81
It was in and about the Martinmas time,   123
It was in and through the window broads   111
It was upon a Lammas night,   113
I've heard them lilting at our yowe-milking,   119
I've seen the smiling   119

J

JOCK O' HAZELDEAN   70
JOHN ANDERSON MY JO   170
JOHN ANDERSON MY JO, JOHN,   171
John Anderson, my jo, John – *polite version*   171
John Anderson, my jo, John, – *rude version*   171
JOHN GRUMLIE   164
John Grumlie swore by the licht o' the moon   165
JOHNNIE COPE   8
JOHNY FAA *OR* THE GYPSIE LADDIE   78
JOY OF MY HEART   184
Joy of my heart, Isle of Moola   185

K

KELVIN GROVE   22

L

LANG HAE WE PARTED BEEN   40
Lang hae we parted been,   40

LEANABH AN AIGH 162
Leanabh an àigh 163
LEEZIE LINDSAY 150
Let us haste to Kelvin Grove, bonnie lassie, O! 23
LORD RONALD 88

M

MAIRI'S WEDDING 152
MARY MORISON 24
McPHERSON'S FAREWELL 90
MINGULAY BOAT SONG 188
MY BOY TAMMY 38
MY DADDY'S A DELVER OF DYKES 63
My Daddy's a Delver of Dykes, 63
My heart is a-breaking, dear Tittie, 63
MY HEART'S IN THE HIGHLANDS 182
My heart's in the Highlands, my heart is not here 183
MY LOVE, SHE'S BUT A LASSIE YET 134
My love she's but a lassie yet, – *Burns's version* 135
My love, she's but a lassie yet, – *Hogg's version* 135
My love was born in Aberdeen 93
MY LOVE'S IN GERMANIE 12
My love's in Germanie, 13
MY MITHER'S AY GLOW'RIN OWRE ME 68
My mither's ay glow'rin owre me, 69
My Patie is a Lover gay, 114
My Sandy gi'ed to me a ring, 59
MY TOCHER'S THE JEWEL 140

N

'N uair bhios mo chàirdean nan cadal, 11

O

O AN YE WERE DEAD, GUDEMAN 168
O an ye were dead, gudeman 169
O CAN YE SEW CUSHIONS? 154
O, can ye sew Cushions and can ye sew
        Sheets? 155
O, CHI, CHI MI NA MOR-BHEANNA 187
O, I AM COME TO THE LOW COUNTRIE 54
O, I am come to the low countrie 54

O Mary, at thy window be, 25
O, meikle thinks my luve o' my beauty. 141
O MY LUVE'S LIKE A RED, RED ROSE 104
O my Luve's like a red, red rose 105
O rowan tree, O rowan tree,
        thou'lt aye be dear o me 191
O THAT I WERE WHERE HELEN LIES 86
O that I were where Helen lies 87
O WALY, WALY UP YON BANK 126
O Waly, Waly, up yon Bank, 126
O when she cam ben she bobbed fu' law, 145
O, where hae ye been, Lord Ronald, my son? 89
Oh, Charlie is my darling, 49
Oh! whither away, my bonnie, bonnie May, 133
One Hogmanay at Glesca Fair 149
ORAN AN T-SAIGHDEIR,
        THE SOLDIER'S SONG 10
OVER THE SEA TO SKYE 53

P

PIBROCH OF DONUIL DHU 4
Pibroch of Donuil Dhu, 5

R

ROBIN ADAIR 60
Robin was a rovin boy 169
ROTHESAY, O 149

S

SCOTS, WHA HAE WI' WALLACE BLED 2
Scots, wha hae wi' Wallace bled, 3
She sat down below a thorn, 98
SHE'S FAIR AND FAUSE THAT CAUSES
        MY SMART 138
She's fair and fause that causes my smart; 139
Should auld acquaintance be forgot, 215
Sing me a song of a lad that is gone, 53
SIR PATRICK SPENCE 96
SORAIDH SLAN LE FIONNAIRIDH! 193
SPEED BONNIE BOAT 52
Speed bonnie boat like a bird on the wing, 53

Step we gaily, on we go   153

T

TAM GLEN   62
THA MI SGITH   56
Tha mi sgìth 's mì leam fhìn,   57
Tha'n latha math, 's an soirbheas ciùin;   193
THE BIRKS OF ABERFELDY   36
THE BIRKS O' ABERGELDIE   37
THE BONNIE BANKS O' LOCH LOMOND   132
THE BONNIE HOUSE O' AIRLIE   80
THE BONNIE EARL O' MURRAY   74
THE BROOM OF COWDENKNOWS   64
THE CAMPBELLS ARE COMIN, OHO! OHO!   6
The Campbells are comin, Oho, Oho!   7
THE DEIL CAM FIDDLIN
        THRO' THE TOWN   198
The deil cam fiddlin thro' the town,   199
The Duke o' Montrose has written to Argyle   81
THE FLOWERS OF THE FOREST   118
THE FOUR MARIES   127
THE GLOOMY NIGHT
        IS GATH'RING FAST   174
The gloomy night is gath'ring fast,   175
THE GREAT SELCHIE OF SULE SKERRY   116
The gypsies came to our Lord's yett,   79
The king sits in Dunfermling toune,   97
THE LAIRD O' COCKPEN   144
The Laird o' Cockpen, he's proud and he's great,   145
THE LAND O' THE LEAL   208
THE MIST-COVERED MOUNTAINS
        OF HOME   187
The piper came to our town,   197
THE PIPER O' DUNDEE   196
THE ROWAN TREE   190
THE SCOTTISH EMIGRANT'S FAREWELL   176
THE SUN RISES BRIGHT IN FRANCE   180
The sun rises bright in France,   181
THE TINKLERS' WADDIN'   146
THE TWA CORBIES   76
THE WHITE COCKADE   92
THE WIFE OF AUCHTERMUCHTY   167
The wind is fair, the day is fine   193

THE WINTER IT IS PAST   124
The winter it is past, and the summer's come at last   125
THERE WAS A LAD WAS BORN IN KYLE   169
There was a wealthy farmer   167
THERE'LL NEVER BE PEACE TILL JAMIE
        COMES HAME   42
Three score o' Nobles rade up the King's ha',   67
THY CHEEK IS O' THE ROSE'S HUE   26
Thy cheek is o' the rose's hue,   27
To the Lords of Convention 'twas Claver'se who spoke   15
TURN YE TO ME   34

V

Vair mi oro van o   107

W

WANDERING WILLIE   178
WEARY FA' YOU DUNCAN GRAY   19
Weary fa' you Duncan Gray,   19
Wha'll buy caller herrin'?   205
Whar hae ye been a' day,   39
What's this dull town to me?   61
WHEN SHE CAM BEN SHE BOBBED   145
Where hae ye been a' the day,   45
WHY SHOULD I SIT AND SIGH?   57
Why should I sit and sigh   57
Why weep ye by the tide, ladye?   71
Will ye gang to the Hielands, Leezie Lindsay?   151
WILL YE NO COME BACK AGAIN?   50
WILLY'S RARE AND WILLY'S FAIR   84
Willy's rare, and Willy's fair,   85
WILT THOU BE MY DEARIE   30
Wilt thou be my dearie?   31

Y

YE BANKS AND BRAES O'
        BONNIE DOON   128
Ye banks and braes o' bonnie Doon,   129
Ye Hielands and ye Lawlands   75
Yestreen the Queen had four Maries,   127
YOUNG WATERS   94